Elasticsearch Blueprints

A practical project-based guide to generating
compelling search solutions using the dynamic
and powerful features of Elasticsearch

Vineeth Mohan

BIRMINGHAM - MUMBAI

Elasticsearch Blueprints

First published: July 2015

Production reference: 1200715

Published by Packt Publishing Ltd.
Livery Place
35 Livery Street
Birmingham B3 2PB, UK.

ISBN 978-1-78398-492-3

www.packtpub.com

Credits

Author
Vineeth Mohan

Reviewers
Kartik Bhatnagar
Tomislav Poljak

Acquisition Editor
Harsha Bharwani

Content Development Editor
Ajinkya Paranjape

Technical Editor
Mrunmayee Patil

Copy Editor
Neha Vyas

Project Coordinator
Harshal Ved

Proofreader
Safis Editing

Indexer
Mariammal Chettiyar

Production Coordinator
Nilesh R. Mohite

Cover Work
Nilesh R. Mohite

About the Author

Vineeth Mohan is an architect and developer. He currently works as the CTO at Factweavers Technologies and is also an Elasticsearch-certified trainer.

He loves to spend time studying emerging technologies and applications related to data analytics, data visualizations, machine learning, natural language processing, and developments in search analytics. He began coding during his high school days, which later ignited his interest in computer science, and he pursued engineering at Model Engineering College, Cochin. He was recruited by the search giant Yahoo! during his college days. After 2 years of work at Yahoo! on various big data projects, he joined a start-up that dealt with search and analytics. Finally, he started his own big data consulting company, Factweavers.

Under his leadership and technical expertise, Factweavers is one of the early adopters of Elasticsearch and has been engaged with projects related to end-to-end big data solutions and analytics for the last few years.

There, he got the opportunity to learn various big-data-based technologies, such as Hadoop, and high-performance data ingress systems and storage. Later, he moved to a start-up in his hometown, where he chose Elasticsearch as the primary search and analytic engine for the project assigned to him.

Later in 2014, he founded Factweavers Technologies along with Jalaluddeen; it is consultancy that aims at providing Elasticsearch-based solutions. He is also an Elasticsearch-certified corporate trainer who conducts trainings in India. Till date, he has worked on numerous projects that are mostly based on Elasticsearch and has trained numerous multinationals on Elasticsearch.

I would like to thank Arun Mohan and my other friends who supported and helped me in completing this book. My unending gratitude goes to the light that guides me.

About the Reviewer

Kartik Bhatnagar is a technical architect at the big data analytics unit of Infosys, Pune. He is passionate about new technologies and the leading development work on Apache Storm and MarkLogic NoSQL. He has 9.5 years of development experience with many fortune clients across countries. He has implemented Elasticsearch engine for a major publishing company in UK. His expertise also includes full-stack Amazon Web Services (AWS). Kartik is also active on the stackoverflow platform and is always eager to help young developers with new technologies.

Kartik is presently working on book based on Storm/Python programming, which is yet to be published.

> I would like to dedicate this book to my niece, Pranika, who will be 6 months old by the time this book gets published. Sincere thanks to my parents; wife, Aditi; and son, Prayrit, for their constant support and love to make the review of this book possible.

www.PacktPub.com

Support files, eBooks, discount offers, and more

For support files and downloads related to your book, please visit www.PacktPub.com.

Did you know that Packt offers eBook versions of every book published, with PDF and ePub files available? You can upgrade to the eBook version at www.PacktPub.com and as a print book customer, you are entitled to a discount on the eBook copy. Get in touch with us at service@packtpub.com for more details.

At www.PacktPub.com, you can also read a collection of free technical articles, sign up for a range of free newsletters and receive exclusive discounts and offers on Packt books and eBooks.

https://www2.packtpub.com/books/subscription/packtlib

Do you need instant solutions to your IT questions? PacktLib is Packt's online digital book library. Here, you can search, access, and read Packt's entire library of books.

Why subscribe?

- Fully searchable across every book published by Packt
- Copy and paste, print, and bookmark content
- On demand and accessible via a web browser

Free access for Packt account holders

If you have an account with Packt at www.PacktPub.com, you can use this to access PacktLib today and view 9 entirely free books. Simply use your login credentials for immediate access.

Table of Contents

Preface

Elasticsearch is a distributed search server similar to Apache Solr with a focus on large datasets, schemaless setup, and high availability. Utilizing the Apache Lucene library (also used in Apache Solr), Elasticsearch enables powerful full-text searches, autocomplete, the "morelikethis" search, multilingual functionality, as well as an extensive search query DSL.

Elasticsearch's schemafree architecture provides developers with built-in flexibility as well as ease of setup. This architecture allows Elasticsearch to index and search unstructured content, making it perfectly suited for both small projects and large big data warehouses—even with petabytes of unstructured data.

This book will enable you to utilize the amazing features of Elasticsearch and build projects to simplify operations on even large datasets. This book starts with the creation of a Google-like web search service, enabling you to generate your own search results. You will then learn how an e-commerce website can be built using Elasticsearch, which will help users search and narrow down the set of products they are interested in. You will explore the most important part of a search—relevancy—based on the various parameters, such as relevance, document collection relevance, user usage pattern, geographic nearness, and document relevance to select the top results.

Next, you will discover how Elasticsearch manages relational content for even complex real-world data. You will then learn the capabilities of Elasticsearch as a strong analytic search platform, which coupled with some visualization techniques can produce real-time data visualization. You will also discover how to improve your search quality and widen the scope of matches using various analyzer techniques. Finally, this book will cover the various geo capabilities of Elasticsearch to make your searches similar to real-world scenarios.

What this book covers

Chapter 1, Google-like Web Search, takes you along the course of building a simple scalable search server. You will learn how to create an index and add some documents to it and you will try out some essential features, such as highlighting and pagination of results. Also, it will cover topics such as setting an analyzer for our text; applying filters to eliminate unwanted characters, such as HTML tags; and so on.

Chapter 2, Building Your Own E-Commerce Solution, covers how to design a scalable e-commerce search solution to generate accurate search results using various filters, such as date-range based and prize-range based filters.

Chapter 3, Relevancy and Scoring, unleashes the power and flexibility of Elasticsearch that will help you implement your own scoring logic.

Chapter 4, Managing Relational Content, covers how to use the document linking or relational features of Elasticsearch.

Chapter 5, Analytics Using Elasticsearch, covers the capability and usage of Elasticsearch in the analytics area with a few use case scenarios.

Chapter 6, Improving the Search Experience, helps you learn how to improve the search quality of a text search. This includes the description of various analyzers and a detailed description of how to mix and match them.

Chapter 7, Spicing Up a Search Using Geo, explores how to use geo information to get the best out of search and scoring.

Chapter 8, Handling Time-based Data, explains the difficulties we face when we use normal indexing in Elasticsearch.

What you need for this book

You will need the following tools to build the projects and execute the queries in this book:

- **cURL**: cURL is an open source command-line tool available in both Windows and Unix. It is widely used to communicate with web interfaces. Since all communication to Elasticsearch can be done through standard REST protocols, we will use cURL throughout the book to communicate with Elasticsearch. The official site for cURL is http://curl.haxx.se/download.html.

- **Elasticsearch**: You need to install Elasticsearch from its official site, `http://www.elasticsearch.org/`. When this book was written, the latest Elasticsearch version available was 1.0.0, so I would recommend that you use this one. The only dependency of Elasticsearch is Java 1.6 or its higher versions. Once you make sure you have installed Java, download the Elasticsearch ZIP file, the installation instructions for which are mentioned in *Chapter 1*, *Google-like Web Search*.

Who this book is for

If you are a developer who has good practical experience in Elasticsearch, Lucene, or Solr and want to know how to implement Elasticsearch in real-world scenarios, then this book is for you.

Conventions

In this book, you will find a number of text styles that distinguish between different kinds of information. Here are some examples of these styles and an explanation of their meaning.

Code words in text, database table names, folder names, filenames, file extensions, pathnames, dummy URLs, user input, and Twitter handles are shown as follows: "Note that for most of the fields that have a string value, such as `sex`, `purposeOfVisit`, and so on, we add the `not_analyzed` field type definition."

A block of code is set as follows:

```
curl -X PUT "http://$hostname:9200/planeticketing" -d '{
    "index": {
        "number_of_shards": 2,
        "number_of_replicas": 1
    }
}'
```

When we wish to draw your attention to a particular part of a code block, the relevant lines or items are set in bold:

```
      "query": "nausea fever"
    }
  },
  "negative": {
    "multi_match": {
      "fields": [
        "title",
        "content"
      ],
```

Any command-line input or output is written as follows:

```
curl -XPOST 'http://localhost:9200/wiki/articles/' -d @India.json
```

New terms and **important words** are shown in bold. Words that you see on the screen, for example, in menus or dialog boxes, appear in the text like this: "Now, take the **Browser** tab in the head UI."

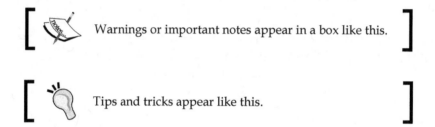

> Warnings or important notes appear in a box like this.

> Tips and tricks appear like this.

Reader feedback

Feedback from our readers is always welcome. Let us know what you think about this book—what you liked or disliked. Reader feedback is important for us as it helps us develop titles that you will really get the most out of.

To send us general feedback, simply e-mail feedback@packtpub.com, and mention the book's title in the subject of your message.

If there is a topic that you have expertise in and you are interested in either writing or contributing to a book, see our author guide at www.packtpub.com/authors.

Customer support

Now that you are the proud owner of a Packt book, we have a number of things to help you to get the most from your purchase.

Downloading the example code

You can download the example code files from your account at `http://www.packtpub.com` for all the Packt Publishing books you have purchased. If you purchased this book elsewhere, you can visit `http://www.packtpub.com/support` and register to have the files e-mailed directly to you.

Errata

Although we have taken every care to ensure the accuracy of our content, mistakes do happen. If you find a mistake in one of our books—maybe a mistake in the text or the code—we would be grateful if you could report this to us. By doing so, you can save other readers from frustration and help us improve subsequent versions of this book. If you find any errata, please report them by visiting `http://www.packtpub.com/submit-errata`, selecting your book, clicking on the **Errata Submission Form** link, and entering the details of your errata. Once your errata are verified, your submission will be accepted and the errata will be uploaded to our website or added to any list of existing errata under the Errata section of that title.

To view the previously submitted errata, go to `https://www.packtpub.com/books/content/support` and enter the name of the book in the search field. The required information will appear under the **Errata** section.

Piracy

Piracy of copyrighted material on the Internet is an ongoing problem across all media. At Packt, we take the protection of our copyright and licenses very seriously. If you come across any illegal copies of our works in any form on the Internet, please provide us with the location address or website name immediately so that we can pursue a remedy.

Please contact us at `copyright@packtpub.com` with a link to the suspected pirated material.

We appreciate your help in protecting our authors and our ability to bring you valuable content.

Questions

If you have a problem with any aspect of this book, you can contact us at questions@packtpub.com, and we will do our best to address the problem.

1
Google-like Web Search

Text search problems are one of the key and common use cases for web-based applications. Developers over the world have been keen to bring an open source solution to this problem. Hence, the Lucene revolution happened. **Lucene** is the heart of most of the search engines that you see today. It basically accepts the text that is to be searched, stores it in an easy searchable form or data structure (inverted index), and then accepts various types of search queries and returns a set of matching results. After the first search revolution, came the second one. Many server-based search solutions, such as Apache SOLR, were built on top of Lucene and marked the second phase of the search revolution. Here, a powerful wrapper was made to interface web users that wanted to index and search text of Lucene. Many powerful tools, notably SOLR, were developed at this stage of revolution. Some of these search frameworks were able to provide document database features too. Then, the next phase of the search revolution came, which is still on-going. The design goal of this phase is provide scaling solutions for the existing stack. **Elasticsearch** is a search and analytic engine that provides a powerful wrapper to Lucene along with an inbuilt document database and provisions various scaling solutions. The document database is also implemented using Lucene. Though competitors of Elasticsearch have some more advanced feature sets, those tools lack the simplicity and the wide range of scalability solutions Elasticsearch offers. Hence, we can see that Elasticsearch is the farthest point to which the search revolution has reached and is the future of text search.

This chapter takes you along the course to build a simple scalable search server. We will see how to create an index and add some documents to it and try out some essential features such as highlighting and pagination of results. Also, we will cover topics such as how to set an analyzer for our text and how to apply filters to eliminate unwanted characters such as HTML tags, and so on.

Here are the important topics that we will cover in this chapter:

- Deploying Elasticsearch
- Concept of the head UI shards and replicas
- Index – type mapping
- Analyzers, filters, and tokenizers
- The head UI

Let's start and explore Elasticsearch in detail.

Deploying Elasticsearch

First, let's download and install the following tools:

- **cURL**: cURL is an open source command-line tool available in both Windows and Unix. It is widely used to communicate with web interfaces. Since all communication to Elasticsearch can be done through standard REST protocols, we will use cURL throughout the book to communicate with Elasticsearch. The official website of cURL is `http://curl.haxx.se/download.html`.

- **Elasticsearch**: You need to install Elasticsearch from its official site `http://www.elasticsearch.org/`. When this book was written, the latest version of Elasticsearch available was 1.0.0, so I would recommend that you use the same version. The only dependency of Elasticsearch is Java 1.6 or its higher versions. Once you make sure that you have Java installed, download the Elasticsearch ZIP file.

First, let's download Elasticsearch:

1. Unzip and place the files in a folder.
2. Next, let's install the Elasticsearch-head plugin. Head is the standard web frontend of the Elasticsearch server. Most of the Elasticsearch operations can be done via a head plugin. To install head, run the following command from the folder where Elasticsearch is installed:

```
bin/plugin -install mobz/elasticsearch-head # (Linux users)
bin\plugin -install mobz/elasticsearch-head # (Windows users)
```

3. You should see a new folder in the `plugins` directory. Open a console and type the following to start Elasticsearch:

```
bin/elasticsearch     #(Linux users)
bin\elasticsearch.bat  #(Windows users)
```

4. The -d command is used to run Elasticsearch in the background rather than the foreground. By running the application in the foreground, we can track the changes taking place in it through the logs spitted in the console. The default behavior is to run in the foreground.

One of the basic design goals of Elasticsearch is its high configurability clubbed with its optimal default configurations that get you started seamlessly. So, all you have to do is start Elasticsearch. You don't have to learn any complex configuration concepts at least to get started. So our search server is up and running now.

To see the frontend of your Elasticsearch server, you can visit `http://localhost:9200/_plugin/head/`.

Communicating with the Elasticsearch server

cURL will be our tool of choice that we will use to communicate with Elasticsearch. Elasticsearch follows a REST-like protocol for its exposed web API. Some of its features are as follows:

- PUT: The HTTP method PUT is used to send configurations to Elasticsearch.

- POST: The HTTP method POST is used to create new documents or to perform a search operation. While successful indexing of documents is done using POST, Elasticsearch provides you with a unique ID that points to the index file.

- GET: The HTTP method GET is used to *retrieve* an already indexed document. Each document has a unique ID called a **doc ID** (short form for document's ID). When we index a document using POST, it provides a document ID, which can be used to retrieve the original document.

- DELETE: The HTTP method DELETE is used to delete documents from the Elasticsearch index. Deletion can be performed based on a search query or directly using the document ID.

To specify the HTTP method in cURL, you can use the -X option, for example, CURL -X POST http://localhost/. JSON is the data format used to communicate with Elasticsearch. To specify the data in cURL, we can specify it in the following forms:

- **A command line**: You can use the -d option to specify the JSON to be sent in the command line itself, for example:

```
curl -X POST 'http://localhost:9200/news/public/'
  -d '{ "time" : "12-10-2010"}
```

- **A file**: If the JSON is too long or inconvenient to be mentioned in a command line, you can specify it in a file or ask cURL to pick the JSON up from the file. You need to use the same `-d` option with a `@` symbol just before the filename, for example:

```
curl -X POST 'http://localhost:9200/news/public/' -d @file
```

Shards and replicas

The concept of **sharding** is introduced in Elasticsearch to provide horizontal scaling. Scaling, as you know, is to increase the capacity of the search engine, both the index size and the query rate (query per second) capacity. Let's say an application can store up to 1,000 feeds and gives reasonable performance. Now, we need to increase the performance of this application to 2,000 feeds. This is where we look for scaling solutions. There are two types of scaling solutions:

- **Vertical scaling**: Here, we add hardware resources, such as more main memory, more CPU cores, or **RAID disks** to increase the capacity of the application.

- **Horizontal scaling**: Here, we add more machines to the system. As in our example, we bring in one more machines and give both the machines 1,000 feeds each. The result is computed by merging the results from both the machines. As both the processes take place in parallel, they won't eat up more time or bandwidth.

Guess what! Elasticsearch can be scaled both horizontally and vertically. You can increase its main memory to increase its performance and you can simply add a new machine to increase its capacity. Horizontal scaling is implemented using the concept of sharding in Elasticsearch. Since Elasticsearch is a distributed system, we need to address our data safety/availability concerns. Using replicas we achieve this. When one replica (size 1) is defined for a cluster with more than one machine, two copies of the entire feed become available in the distributed system. This means that even if a single machine goes down, we won't lose data and at the same time. The load would be distributed somewhere else. One important point to mention here is that the default number of shards and replicas are generally sufficient and also, we have the provision to change the replica number later on.

This is how we create an index and pass the number of shards and replicas:

```
curl -X PUT "localhost:9200/news" -d '{
"settings": {
"index": {
"number_of_shards": 2,
```

```
"number_of_replicas": 1
    }
  }
}'
```

A few things to be noted here are:

- Adding more primary shards will increase the write throughout the index
- Adding more replicas will increase the durability of the index and the read throughout, at the cost of disk space

Index-type mapping

An index is a grouping logic where feeds of the same type are encapsulated together. A type is a sub grouping logic under index. To create a type under index, you need to decide on a type name. As in our case, we take the index name as news and the type name as public. We created the index in the previous step and now we need to define the data types of the fields that our data hold in the type mapping section.

Check out the sample given next. Here, the date data type takes the time format to be yyyy/MM/dd HH:mm:ss by default:

```
curl -X PUT "localhost:9200/news/public/_mapping" -d '{
"public" :{
"properties" :{
"Title" : {"type" : "string" },
"Content": {"type" : "string" },
"DOP": {"type" : "date" }
}
}
}'
```

Once we apply mapping, certain aspects of it such as new field definitions can be updated. However, we can't update certain other aspects such as changing the type of a field or changing the assigned analyzer. So, we now know how to create an index and add necessary mappings to the index we created. There is another important thing that you must take care of while indexing your data, that is, the analysis of our data. I guess you already know the importance of analysis. In simple terms, analysis is the breaking down of text into an elementary form called **tokens**. This tokenization is a must and has to be given serious consideration. Elasticsearch has many built-in analyzers that do this job for you. At the same time, you are free to deploy your own custom analyzers as well if the built-in analyzers do not serve your purpose. Let's see analysis in detail and how we can define analyzers for fields.

Setting the analyzer

Analyzers constitute an important part of indexing. To understand what analyzers do, let's consider three documents:

- **Document1 (tokens)**: { This , is , easy }
- **Document2 (tokens)**: { This , is , fast }
- **Document3 (tokens)**: { This , is , easy , and , fast }

Here, terms such as This, is, as well as and are not relevant keywords. The chances of someone wanting to search for such words are very less, as these words don't contribute to the facts or context of the document. Hence, it's safe to avoid these words while indexing or rather you should avoid making these words searchable.

So, the tokenization would be as follows:

- **Document1 (tokens)**: { easy }
- **Document2 (tokens)**: { fast }
- **Document3 (tokens)**: { easy , fast }

Words such as the, or, as well as and are referred to as **stop words**. In most cases, these are for grammatical support and the chances that someone will search based on these words are slim. Also, the analysis and removal of stop words is very much language dependent. The process of selecting/transforming the searchable tokens from a document while indexing is called **analyzing**. The module that facilitates this is called an analyzer. The analyzer we just discussed is a stop word analyzer. By applying the right analyzer, you can minimize the number of searchable tokens and hence get better performance results.

There are three stages through which you can perform an analysis:

- **Character filters**: Filtering is done at character level before processing for tokens. A typical example of this is an HTML character filter. We might give an HTML to be indexed to Elasticsearch. In such instances, we can provide the HTML CHAR filter to do the work.
- **Tokenizers**: The logic to break down text into tokens is depicted in this state. A typical example of this is whitespace tokenizers. Here, text is broken down into tokens by splitting the text based on the white space occurrence.
- **Token filters**: On top of the previous process, we apply a token filter. In this stage, we filter tokens to match our requirement. The length token filter is a typical token filter. A token filter of type length removes words which are too long or too short for the stream.

Here is a flowchart that depicts this process:

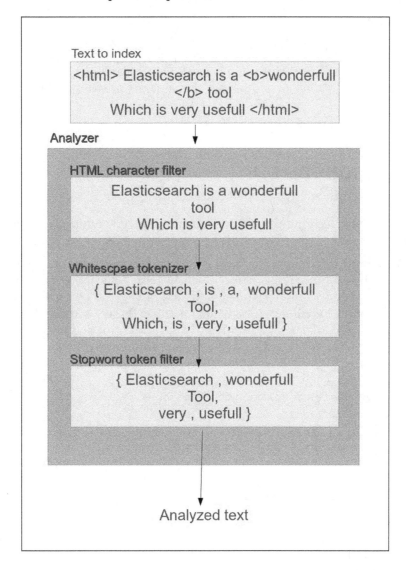

It should be noted that any number of such components can be incorporated in each stage. A combination of these components is called an analyzer. To create an analyzer out of the existing components, all we need to do is add the configuration to our Elasticsearch configuration file.

Types of character filters

The following are the different types of character filters:

- **HTML stripper**: This strips the HTML tags out of the text.
- **Mapping char filter**: Here, you can ask Elasticsearch to convert a set of characters or strings to another set of characters or strings. The options are as follows:

```
"mappings" : ["ph=>f", "qu=>q"]
```

Types of tokenizers

The following are different types of tokenizers:

- **The whitespace tokenizer**: A tokenizer of this type whitespace divides text at whitespace.
- **The shingle tokenizer**: There are instances where you want to search for text with two consecutive words, such as Latin America. In conventional searches, Latin would be a token and America would be a token, so you won't be able to boil down to the text that has these words next to each other. In the shingle tokenizer, *n* number of tokens are grouped into a single token. Token generation for a 2Gram tokenizer would be as follows:

```
"Latin America is a great place to go in summer"
  => { "Latin America" ,"America is" , "is a" , "a great" ,
  "great place" , "place to" , "to go" , "go in" ,
  "in summer" }
```

- **The lowercase tokenizer**: This converts text into lowercase, thereby decreasing the index size.

Types of token filters

The following are the different types of token filters:

- **The stop word token filter**: A set of words are recognized as stop words. This includes words like "is", "the", as well as "and" that don't add facts to the statement, but support the statement grammatically. A stop word token filter removes the stop words and hence helps to conduct more meaningful and efficient searches.

- **The length token filter**: With this, we can filter out tokens that have length greater than a configured value.

- **The stemmer token filter**: Stemming is an interesting concept. There are words such as "learn", "learning", "learnt", and so on that refer to the same word, but then are in different tenses. Here, we only need to index the actual word "learn" for any of its tenses. This is what a stemmer token filter does. It translates different tenses of the same word to the actual word.

Creating your own analyzer

Now, let's create our own analyzer and apply it on an index. I want to make an analyzer that strips out HTML tags before indexing. Also, there should not be any differentiation between lowercase and uppercase while searching. In short, the search is case insensitive. We are not interested in searching words such as "is" and "the", which are stop words. Also, we are not interested in words that have more than 900 characters. The following are the settings that you need to paste in the config/Elasticsearch.yml file to create this analyzer:

```
index :
analysis :
analyzer :
myCustomAnalyzer :
tokenizer : smallLetter
filter : [lowercase, stopWord]
char_filter : [html_strip]
tokenizer :
smallLetter:
type : standard
max_token_length : 900
filter :
stopWord:
type : stop
stopwords : ["are" , "the" , "is"]
```

Here, I named my analyzer myCustomAnalyzer. By adding the character filter html_strip, all HTML tags are removed out of the stream. A filter called stopWord is created, where we define the stop words. If we don't mention the stop words, those are taken from the default set. The smallLetter tokenizer removes all the words that have more than 900 characters.

Readymade analyzers

A combination of character filters, token filters, and tokenizers is called an analyzer. You can make your own analyzer using these building blocks, but then, there are readymade analyzers that work well in most of the use cases. A **Snowball Analyzer** is an analyzer of the type snowball that uses the standard tokenizer with the standard filter, lowercase filter, stop filter, and snowball filter, which is a stemming filter.

Here is how you can pass the analyzer setting to Elasticsearch:

```
curl -X PUT "http://localhost:9200/wiki" -d '{
  "index" : {
    "number_of_shards" : 4,
    "number_of_replicas" : 1 ,
    "analysis":{
      "analyzer":{
        "content" : {
          "type" : "custom",
          "tokenizer" : "standard",
          "filter" : ["lowercase" , "stop" , "kstem"],
          "char_filter" : ["html_strip"]
        }
      }
    }
  }
}'
```

Having understood how we can create an index and define field mapping with the analyzers, we shall go ahead and index some Wikipedia documents. For quick demonstration purpose, I have created a simple Python script to make some JSON documents. I am trying to create corresponding JSON files for the wiki pages for the following countries:

- China
- India
- Japan
- The United States
- France

Here is the script written in Python if you want to use it. This takes as input two command-line arguments: the first one is the title of the page and the second is the link:

```python
import urllib2
import json
import sys

link = sys.argv[2]
htmlObj = { "link" : link ,
    "Author" : "anonymous" ,
    "timestamp" : "09-02-2014 14:16:00",
    "Title" : sys.argv[1]
    }
response = urllib2.urlopen(link)
htmlObj['html'] = response.read()
print json.dumps(htmlObj , indent=4)
```

Let's assume the name of the Python file is `json_generator.py`. The following is how we execute it:

Python json_generator.py https://en.wikipedia.org/wiki/France > France.json'.

Now, we have a JSON file called `France.json` that has a sample data we are looking for.

I assume that you generated JSON files for each country that we mentioned. As seen earlier, indexing a document once it is created is simple. Using the script shown next, I created the index and defined the mappings:

```
curl -X PUT "http://localhost:9200/wiki" -d '{
    "index" : {
  "number_of_shards" : 4,
  "number_of_replicas" : 1 ,
      "analysis":{
        "analyzer":{
      "content" : {
        "type" : "custom",
        "tokenizer" : "standard",
        "filter" : ["lowercase" , "stop" , "kstem"],
        "char_filter" : ["html_strip"]
```

```
              }
           }
         }
       }

   }'

curl -X PUT "http://localhost:9200/wiki/articles/_mapping" -d '{
  "articles" :{
    "_all" : {"enabled" : true },
    "properties" :{
    "Title" : { "type" : "string" , "Analyzer":"content" ,
      "include_in_all" : true},
    "link" : { "type" : "string" ,  "include_in_all" : false ,
      "index" : "no" },
    "Author" : { "type" : "string" , "include_in_all" : false    },
    "timestamp" : { "type" : "date", "format" : "dd-MM-yyyy
      HH:mm:ss" , "include_in_all" : false },
    "html" : { "type" : "string" ,"Analyzer":"content" ,
      "include_in_all" : true }
    }
  }
}'
```

Once this is done, documents can be indexed like this. I assume that you have the file `India.json`. You can index it as:

```
curl -XPOST 'http://localhost:9200/wiki/articles/' -d @India.json
```

Index all the documents likewise.

Using phrase query to search

We added some documents to the index that we created. Now, let's examine some ways to query our data. Elasticsearch provides many types of queries to query our indexed documents. Of all the ones available, the simple query string query is a great place to start. The main advantage of this query is that it will never throw an exception. Also, a simple query string query discards the invalid parts of the query.

It mostly covers what is expected from most of the search engines. It takes OR of all the terms present in the query text, though we can change this behavior to AND. Also, it recognizes all Boolean keywords in the query text and performs the search accordingly. For details, you can look through `http://lucene.apache.org/core/2_9_4/queryparsersyntax.html`.

To query an Elasticsearch index, we must create a JSON query. A simple JSON query is shown here:

```
{
"query": {
    "simple_query_string": {
      "query": "sms",
      "fields": [
        "_all"
      ]
    }
  }
}
```

The screenshot of how a query is passed and the response is received in the head UI is shown as follows:

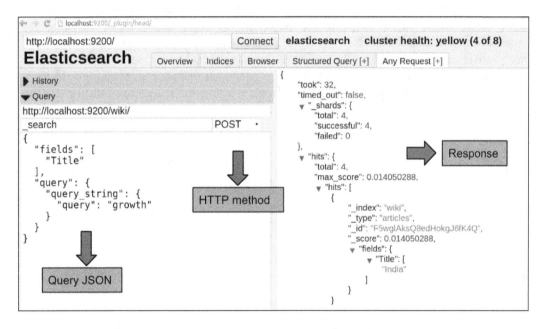

The explanation of the field's result is as follows:

- `took`: This is the time taken by Elasticsearch in milliseconds to perform the search on the index.

- `hits`: This array contains the records of the first 10 documents that matched.

- `_id`: This is a unique ID that refers to that document.

- _score: This is a number that determines how closely the search parameter you provided matched this particular result.

- _source: When we give Elasticsearch a feed to document, it stores the original feed separately. On a document match, we receive this stored document as the _source field.

Using the highlighting feature

When we searched for a record, what we got was its actual data or _source. However, this information is not what we actually need in search results. Instead, we want to extract the text out of the content, which helps the users to better understand the context where the text was matched in the document. For example, say the user searched for the word cochin, he would like to check whether the document speaks about the city Cochin or the cochin bank in Japan. Seeing other words around the word cochin will further help the user to judge whether that is the document he/she is searching for. Elasticsearch provides you with fragments of text on request for the highlighted text. Each fragment has the matched text and some words around it. As there can be any number of matched queries in the same document, you would be provided an array of fragments per document, where each fragment would contain the context of the matched query.

Here is how we ask Elasticsearch to provide the highlighted text:

```
{
"query" : {...},
"highlight" : {
"fields" : {
"Content" : {}
}
}
}
```

Under fields, you need to specify which all fields' highlighted text is required by you. In this example, we require the Content field.

Now, let's see another awesome feature that Elasticsearch offers. You would have noticed in Google search that the matched text in the highlighted fragments is shown in bold. Elasticsearch provides support for this as follows:

```
{
"query" : {...},
"highlight" : {
"pre_tags" : ["<b>"],
"post_tags" : ["</b>"],
```

```
"fields" : {
"Content" : {}
}
}
}
```

Here, you can mention the pre tag and post tag. To get the matched text in bold, simply input pre tag as <b> and post tag as </b>. By default, the <em>   </em> tags are provided. The maximum number of fragments and maximum number of words per fragment are also configurable.

Pagination

While searching, users can't view all the results at once. They like to see one batch at a time. Usually, a single batch contains 10 matched documents, as in Google search results, where each page contains 10 search results. This also gives us an advantage over the search engine as it need not send all the results back at once. The following is how we use pagination in Elasticsearch. Let's say that we are interested in seeing only five results at a time, then to get the first page, we have to use the following parameters:

- size = 5 (defaults to 10).

- from = 0, 5, 10, 15, 20 (defaults to 0). This depends on the page number you need.

Also, it should be noted that the total number of pages can be calculated from count/_size. Sample query for the page 5 of the search result where we show 5 results at a time:

```
{
"from" : 4 ,
"size" : 5,
"query": {… }   }
```

This is how the complete query looks, which enables pagination and highlighting:

```
{
  "from": 0,
  "size": 10,
  "query": {
    "simple_query_string": {
      "query": "china",
      "fields": [
        "_all"
      ]
```

```
        }
    },
    "highlight": {
      "fields": {
        "html": {
          "pre_tags": [
            "<p>"
          ],
          "post_tags": [
            "</p>"
          ],
          "fragment_size": 10,
          "number_of_fragments": 3
        }
      }
    }
}
```

The head UI explained

When you open the head page, you see a UI that lists all the indexes and all the
information related to it. Also, by looking at the tabs to the left, you know how
well your cluster is doing, as shown in the following figure:

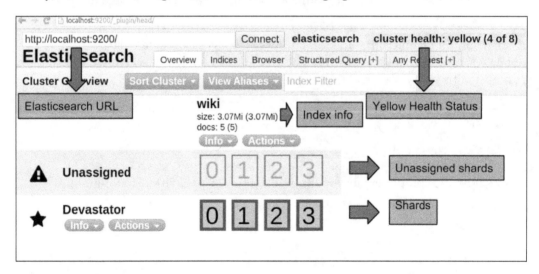

Now, take the **Browser** tab in the head UI. You will see all the feeds you index here.
Note that it shows only the first 10 indexed feeds.

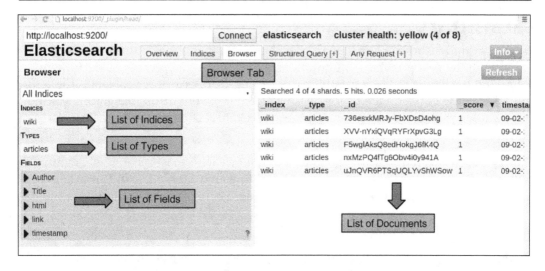

Now, on selecting one of your feeds, a nice model window appear, showing you the following view:

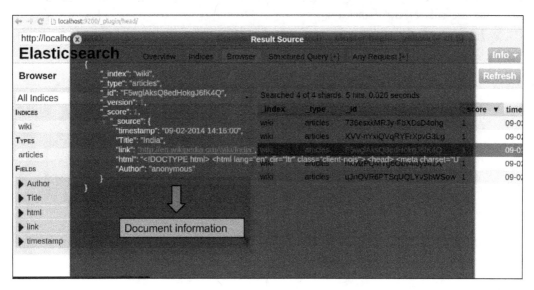

In this chapter, we looked at how we can deploy Elasticsearch. We had a quick look at of how to set an analyzer and index some documents. Then, we attempted to search for a document we indexed. We will look at how pagination and highlighting work in later sections of this book.

Summary

Kick starting Elasticsearch is much easier than any other open source projects. It ships with the best possible configurations, which make the process of starting this easy, and it ships with the most optimistic settings for performance. Hence, the initial learning curve on the user side is reduced. We went through a getting started that was easy; and discussed some of the architectural choices, which make this application truly distributed.

Though Elasticsearch head is a good tool to interact with Elasticsearch. There are other choices, such as Sense (packed with Elasticsearch Marvel), KOPF, and so on, which can also be used for the same purpose. There is a wide variety of ways in which we can use analyzers to improve a user's search experience. A separate chapter is dedicated to this in this book.

In the next chapter, you will learn how you can effectively use Elasticsearch to build an e-commerce application. Elasticsearch is a natural fit to build an e-commerce application. Search over structured and unstructured data, pagination, scoring, aggregation, filtering, and highlighting makes Elasticsearch an ideal backend for e-commerce-related applications.

2
Building Your Own E-Commerce Solution

In the first chapter, we discussed how to add documents to an Elasticsearch instance as well as how to create the fields and decide on an analyzer. All these are steps to get you started. The next two chapters help you to get accustomed to the process of creating an e-commerce search solution. E-commerce revolutionized ways to shop, and the convenience that such a trading system provides attracted people very much. Amazon, eBay, and Flipkart are all pioneers in this field. Elasticsearch offers wonderful support to build such platforms, where you can display what you have. There are numerous techniques that can push the user experience even higher, which can eventually reflect on the overall performance of such a system. This is what we deal with in this chapter. Take a look at the contents of this chapter:

- Building the document
- A query or filter — the right choice
- A date-range-based filter
- A prize-range-based filter
- A category-based filter/facet
- Building a sample e-commerce document

Data modeling in Elasticsearch

Data is modeled in documents in Elasticsearch. This means a single item irrespective of whether it is an entity like a company, country, or product has to be modeled as a single document. A document can contain any number of fields and values associated with it. This information is modeled around the JSON format that helps us to express the behavior of our data using arrays, objects, or simple values.

 Elasticsearch is schemaless, which means that you can index a document to Elasticsearch before you create its index or mapping. Elasticsearch guesses the best type for each field value.

Inherently, JSON supports formats such as string, numbers, object, array, and even Boolean. Elasticsearch adds various other formats on top of it, such as the date, IP and so on. You will find the list of such supported types in the following table. The use of date types to store date values will help us do effective date-specific operations, such as date range and aggregation on top of it. This can't be done if we use the default string type. The same goes for other custom types, such as IP, geo_point, and so on.

Type	Definition
String	Text
Integer	32-bit integers
Long	64-bit integers
Float	IEEE floats
Double	Double precision floats
Boolean	True or false
Date	Date/Time stored as epoch
geo_point	Latitude/Longitude
Null	Null value
Ipv4	IP version 4

It is necessary that you let Elasticsearch know what type of data that particular field will hold. We saw how to pass the type configuration to an Elasticsearch instance. Besides that, you can use various other configurations to fine-tune your overall search performance. We may see a few configurations in due course. However, learning all these configuration parameters is worthwhile and will be useful when you try to fine-tune your search performance.

Imagine yourself in a scenario where you are in need and want to build a shopping application. The first step to build such an application is to get your product information indexed. Here, it would be best to model a document around a single product. Hence, a single document represents all the data associated with a product, such as its name, description, date of manufacture, and so on.

First, let's create the index:

```
curl -X PUT "http://localhost:9200/products" -d '{
    "index": {
        "number_of_shards": 1,
        "number_of_replicas": 1
    }
}'
```

Here, we assume that the Elasticsearch instance runs on the local machine or rather, the localhost. We create an index called `products` with one shard and one replica. This means that our data won't be partitioned across shards; instead, a single shard will handle it. This means that in future, it's not possible to scale out across new machines added to the cluster. A replica of one makes sure that a copy of the shard is maintained elsewhere too.

 More shards when distributed in various hardware will increase the index/write throughout. More replicas increase the search/read throughout.

Now, let's make the mapping.

Here, `products` is the index and `product` is the type:

```
curl -X PUT "http://localhost:9200/products/product/
  _mapping" -d ' {
    "product":{
        "properties":{
            "name":{
                "type":"string"
            },
            "description":{
                "type":"string"
            },
            "dateOfManufactoring":{
                "type":"date",
                "format":"YYYY-MM-dd"
            },
            "price":{
```

```
                    "type":"long"
              },
              "productType":{
                    "type":"string",
                    "include_in_all":"false",
                    "index":"not_analyzed"
// By setting the attribute index as not_analyzed ,
// we are asking Elasticsearch not to analyze the string.
//This is required to do aggregation effectively.

              },
              "totalBuy":{
                    "type":"long",
                    "include_in_all":"false"
              },
              "imageURL":{
                    "type":"string",
                    "include_in_all":"false",
                    "index":"no"
// As we won't normally search URL's , we are setting
//the index to no. This means that this field is
//not searchable but retrievable.
                    }
              }
        }
}'
```

Here, we modeled the information on a single product as a document and created various fields to hold that information. Let's see what these fields are and how we treat them:

- name: This field stores the name of our product. We should be able to search by this name even if we provide a single word for it. So, if the name is Lenovo laptops, even if the user gives only the word Lenovo, this document should match. Hence, it has to go through a process called **analysis**, where tokens qualified to represent this string are selected. We will talk about this in detail later. However, we need to understand that this process happens by default, until you configure otherwise.

- description: This field holds the description of the product and should be treated the same as the name field.

- `dateOfManufactoring`: This is the date on which this product was manufactured. Here, if we don't declare this field as a date, it would be assumed to be a string. The problem with this approach is that when we try to do range selection on this field, rather than looking into the date value, it looks at its lexicographical value (that is computed based on an alphabetical or dictionary order), which will give us a wrong result. This means that a date search between two date ranges won't give accurate results in the case of a string type. Hence, we need to declare this field as a date and it stores this field in the Unix epoch format. But wait! There are numerous formats of date. How will Elasticsearch understand the right format and parse out the right date value? For that, you need to provide the format as a format attribute. Using this format, the date string is parsed and the epoch value is computed. Furthermore, all queries and aggregations are solved and take place through this parsed date value and hence, we get the actual results.

- `price`: This field has the price value as a number.

- `productType`: This field stores the product type such as `Laptop`, `Tab`, and so on, as a string. However, this string is not broken so that aggregation results make sense. It has to be noted here that when we make this field `not_analyzed`, it's not searchable on a token level. What this means is that if the product type is `Large Laptop`, the search query of the word `Laptop` won't give you a match, but rather, the exact word `Large Laptop` alone will give you a match. However, through this approach, aggregation works neatly.

- `totalBuy`: This is a field maintained by us to track the number of items bought for this field.

- `imageURL`: We store the image of this product in external image database and provide the URL to access it. As we are not going to conduct a search or aggregate this field, it's safe to disable the index for this field. This means that this field won't be searchable, but will be retrievable.

We have already learned how to index data in Elasticsearch. Assume that you indexed the information you wished to. If you would like to see the overview of your index, you can install Elasticsearch-head as a simple frontend to your index. This is how a sample search result looks like after indexing the information:

```
{

    "took": 87,
    "timed_out": false,
    "_shards": {
        "total": 1,
        "successful": 1,
        "failed": 0
```

```
        },
    "hits": {
        "total": 4,
        "max_score": 1,
        "hits": [
            {
                "_index": "products",
                "_type": "product",
                "_id": "CD5BR19RQ3mD3MdNhtCq9Q",
                "_score": 1,
                "_source": {
                    "name": "Lenovo A1000L Tablet",
                    "description": "Lenovo Ideatab A1000
                        Tablet (4GB, WiFi, Voice Calling), Black",
                    "dateOfManufactoring": "2014-01-01",
                    "prize": 6699,
                    "totalBuy": 320,
                    "productType": "Tablet",
                    "imageURL":
                        "www.imageDB.com/urlTolenovoTablet.jpg"
                }
            }
        ]
    }
}
```

The greatest advantage of using Elasticsearch is the level at which you can control your data. The flexible schema lets you define your own ways to deal with your information. So, the user can have absolute freedom to define the fields and the types that the user's virtual document would hold (in our case, a particular product).

Choosing between a query and a filter

The basic idea of a search is to narrow down on a subset of documents that you have. In the Elasticsearch context, this means that based on various conditions, you might want to select a set of documents from an index or a set of index. A query and filter facilitate this for you.

If you have already gone through the reference guide or some other documentation of Elasticsearch, you might have noticed that the same set of operations might be available for both queries and filters. So, what are the differentiating factors of a query and filter even when the set of operations given by them are almost the same? Let's find out.

In a query, a matched document can be a better match than another matched document. In a filter, all the matched documents are treated equally.

This means that there is a way to score or rank a document matched against a query to another document match. This is done by computing a score value that tells you how good a match a particular document is against a query. If the query is a better match, give a higher score and if it's a lesser match, give a lesser score. This way, we can identify the best matches and use that in the paging.

For an e-commerce site, the success is decided on what percentage of input traffic is converted to purchase. A customer searches for something he/she is interested in buying and if we can't show him the most relevant results in the first page itself, then the chance of converting the search into a purchase would be slim. Mostly, none of the customers would look at the second page or subsequent pages for best options. They will assume that the products in further pages are of lesser importance than the current page and will drop the search there. Hence, we have to use queries to make our result order more relevant to the user.

But wait, what are the advantages of filters? Let's explore them.

 Filters don't compute the matched score per document and hence, they are faster. The results are also cached, which means that from the second search, the speed will be really good.

So, for structured searches, such as a date range, number range, and so on, where scoring doesn't come in picture, filters is our man. It has to be noted that filters can be used in many areas. They are:

- **Queries**: A filter can be used for querying. Note that like a query has a separate section called query in a Query **DSL** (**domain-specific language**), there is no separate section for filters. Rather, you need to embed your filter inside the `constant_score` query type or the `filtered_query` type.

- **Scoring**: Elasticsearch provides you a query type called the `function_score` query. Using the capabilities of this query type, we can use a filter and boost the score based on the filter match.

- **A post filter**: This is applied to the search results, but not to the input of the aggregation. This means that even though the scope of aggregation is its query, we can modify this behavior by adding the post filter. Post filters are only applied to search results or hits and not to the aggregation input.

- **Aggregations**: We can also specify filters inside aggregations to filter documents inside a bucket.

A very interesting point to note here is that filters are cached and used independent of the context. This means that once you use a filter in a query and reuse the same filter in an aggregation or post filter, the same cache is hit instead of computing the results.

> Hence, make sure that you always use a mixture of filters and queries, where constraints are as much moved to filters depending on the situation. This will allow unwanted computation of scores.

Searching your documents

To search we use a large set of documents and our interest here lies only in a subset of this document set. This can be based on a set of constraints and conditions. A search does not stop here. You might be interested in getting a snapshot view of your query result. In our case, if the user searches for `dell`, he/she might be interested in seeing different unique product types and their document count. This is called an aggregation. Through this, we enhance our search experience and make it more explorable. Here, we try to discover various querying options through which we can express our requirement and communicate the same to Elasticsearch.

In our search application, we expose a search box that can be used for a search. We abstract out information about which field is searched or what is the precedence of the fields that we search. Let's see the query types that would be best for this search box.

A match query

A match query is the ideal place to start your query. It can be used to search many field types, such as a number, string, or even date. Let's see how we can use this to provide the search input box. Let's assume that a user fired a search against the keyword `laptop`. It does make sense to search on the field's name and description for this keyword and there is no sense to do the same for price or date fields.

> Elasticsearch, by default, stores an additional search field called `_all`, which is an aggregated field over all the field values in that document. Hence, to do a document-level search, it's good to use `_all`.

A simple match query in all the fields for a word `laptop` is as follows:

```
{
  "query": {
    "match": {
      "_all": "laptop"
    }
  }
}
```

Wait, won't we be using the `_all` search on the date and price fields too? Which we don't intent to… not in this case. Remember, we search `include_in_all` as `false` for all fields other than the name and description fields. This will make sure that these field values won't flow to `_all`.

Sweet, we are able to search on the string fields that make sense to us and we get neat results. However, now, the requirement from the management has changed. Rather than treating the name field and description field with equal precedence, I would rather like to give weightage to the name field over description. This means that for a document match, if the word is present in the name field, make that document more relevant over a document, where the match that worked is only on the field description. Let's see how we can achieve it using a variance of a match query.

Multifield match query

A multifield match query has the provision to search on multiple fields rather than a single field. Wait, it doesn't stop here. You can also give precedence or importance to each field along with it. This helps us to tell Elasticsearch to treat certain field matches better than others:

```
{
    "query": {
        "multi_match": {
            "query": "laptop",
            "fields": [
            "name^2",
            "description"
            ]
        }
    }
}
```

Here, we ask Elasticsearch to match the word `laptop` on both the field name and description, but give greater relevancy to a match on the field name over a match on description field.

Let's consider the following documents:

- Document A:
    - **Name**: Lenovo laptop
    - **Description**: This is a great product with very high rating from Lenovo

- Document B:
    - **Name**: Lenovo bags
    - **Description**: These are great laptop bags with very high rating from Lenovo

A search on the word `laptop` will yield a better match on Document A rather than Document B, which makes perfectly good sense in the real-world scenario.

Aggregating your results

Next, when I search for Lenovo, I would like to see different product types associated with it. This is more like making a report out of the results, but then, as this makes your data more explorable and easy to understand, it's safe to see this as enhancing search capabilities.

Hence, whenever I search for something, I want to see the following reports on my query results or rather, an aggregate of my results in the following information:

- Different types of `productType`
- The number of products in various predefined price ranges
- The number of documents per year based on manufacturing dates

For this, we need to build different aggregations to capture these reports.

 It's very important to understand that the score of aggregation is the query. This means that the aggregations would only be done on those documents that match the query.

The format in which we should provide aggregations is as follows:

```
{
    "query" : { ...},
    "aggregations" : {
        "aggregationNameA" : {
            "aggregationType" : {
                <Aggregation type specific information> },
        }
    },
    "aggregationNameB" : {
        "aggregationType" : {
            <Aggregation type specific information> },
        }
    },
    { .... }
}
```

Once we fire a search request with this JSON, we can retrieve our results in the following format:

```
{
    "took" : 21 ,
    ....
}
```

 We identify the results of the individual aggregation request using the aggregation name we gave in the query.

Terms aggregation

Terms aggregation is usually done on string field types, which means that this is very handy to retrieve statistics on terms. Like in our case, the number of different unique values for the productType and the number of documents in which each terms are occurring.

Filter your results based on a date range

With a fair idea in mind of when to use your filter and when to opt for a query, let's think of some scenarios and see how Elasticsearch enables filtering at its best. Filtering by a date range, prize, or department often pops up in use cases in an e-commerce view. Look at the left-hand side of the following figure:

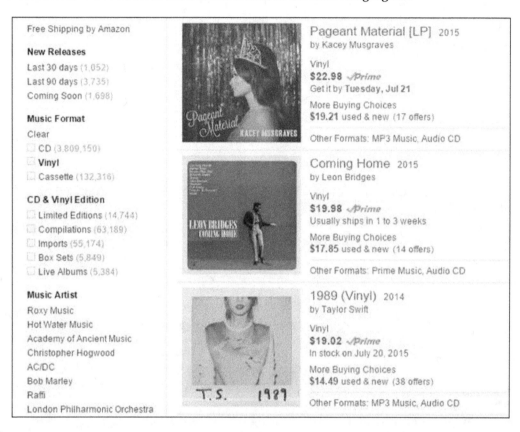

Checking for new arrivals or selecting an old classic song from a library may need a date-range-based filtering mechanism. Elasticsearch provides inbuilt facilities to do filtering by providing a date range filter. A term filter does the same thing for strings, which can be anything for example, a department or category. A numeric filter filters numerals and can be used for prizes and so on.

This snippet shows how you can implement a date-range-based filtering in Elasticsearch:

```
{
"query" :
{ "filtered" :
  { "query" :
```

```
    { "text" : { "content" : "any keywords to match" }
  },
  "filter" :
{ "numeric_range" :
  { "date" :
    { "lt" : "2011-02-01", "gte" : "2011-01-01"
    }
  }
  }
  }
```

These are the parameters taken in a range filter that you may use to specify range offsets:

Parameters	Meaning
gte	Greater than or equal to
gt	Greater than
lte	Less than or equal to
lt	Less than

Implementing a prize range filter

Now, let's move on and see how to implement a prize range filter as seen in some e-commerce websites. Consider the following screenshot of an e-commerce site:

In the preceding screenshot, you can see a price range filter on the left-hand side tab. By clicking on or specifying the price ranges, the products that fall within that range would be displayed. This is nothing but a numeric range filter.

The implementation of a numeric range filter is almost similar to the date range filter in Elasticsearch. The following code snippet shows how to implement a numeric range filter. Here is the sample; assume that you have an age field that is numeric in nature:

```
{
    "filtered" : {
        "filter" : {
            "range" : {
                "age" : {
                    "gte": 10,
                    "lte": 20
                }
            }
        }
    }
}
```

After reading the implementation of filters, which is to be followed, you would understand the snippet completely. For time being, we have just showed you how to implement a filter in a numeric field in Elasticsearch.

The same parameters that are shown in the previous table are applied here as well.

Implementing a category filter

Normally, the category fields are of the type string. We need to index this unanalyzed field to match the exact term. In fact, Elasticsearch uses a term filter for the purpose of matching strings:

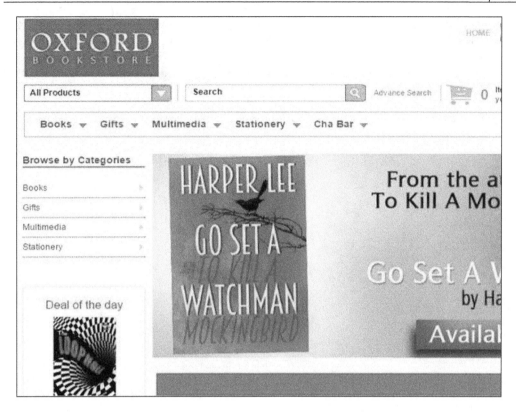

The following snippet shows you how to use a terms filter:

```
{
    "filtered" : {
        "filter" : {
            "term" : {
                "category" : "Books"

            }
        }
    }
}
```

Implementation of filters in Elasticsearch

This section sheds some light on the implementation of filters in Elasticsearch. All filters are not the same. We will see how each one differs from another and how we can implement these with Elasticsearch. First, let's see all the three implementation types of filters in Elasticsearch.

We have already showed you the most basic type of usage of a filter in the previous examples. You would have noticed the term constant score or filtered every time we used a filter. These are queries and they wrap the filter inside and apply it against the normal query's result. This is the first type of filter implementation of Elasticsearch.

Note that the filtered/constant score implementation of filters will affect both the results of the query and aggregations; some of the examples are shown as follows:

```
curl -XPOST 'http://localhost:9200/products/_search?pretty' -d '{
    "aggregations": {
      "department": {
        "terms": {
          "field": "color"
        }
      }
    },
    "query": {
      "filtered": {
        "query": {
          "match": {
            "description": "dell"
          }
        },
        "filter": {
          "term": {
            "productType": "Laptop"
          }
        }
      }
    }
}'
```

The output of the preceding query is as follows:

```
{
  "took" : 250,
  "timed_out" : false,
  "_shards" : {
    "total" : 1,
    "successful" : 1,
    "failed" : 0
  },
  "hits" : {
    "total" : 2,
    "max_score" : 0.48288077,
```

```
"hits" : [ {
  "_index" : "products",
  "_type" : "product",
  "_id" : "-B0YVCS6R1iXOqhHNKRcJQ",
  "_score" : 0.48288077,
  "_source":{    "name" : "Dell Vostro 3546 Laptop",
    "description" : "Dell Vostro 3546 Laptop with Laptop Bag",
    "dateOfManufactoring" : "2013-05-06",    "prize" : 25688,
    "totalBuy" : 20 ,    "color" : "Yellow",    "productType" :
    "Laptop",    "imageURL" :
    "www.imageDB.com/urlToDellVostroLaptop.jpg"}
}, {
  "_index" : "products",
  "_type" : "product",
  "_id" : "J-41WEDDQPaondNpQtbFLQ",
  "_score" : 0.40240064,
  "_source":{    "name" : "Dell Inspiron Laptop",
  "description" : "Dell Inspiron 3541 Black 15.6
  inch Laptop without Laptop Bag",    "dateOfManufactoring" :
  "2012-04-01",    "prize" : 19990,    "totalBuy" : 334 ,
  "color" : "Grey",    "productType" : "Laptop",    "imageURL"
  : "www.imageDB.com/urlToDellInspironLaptop.jpg"}
} ]
},
"aggregations" : {
  "department" : {
    "buckets" : [ {
      "key" : "Grey",
      "doc_count" : 1
    }, {
      "key" : "Yellow",
      "doc_count" : 1
    } ]
  }
}
}
```

Searching with multiple conditions

Often, we find ourselves in a position where we need to search with more than one criterion, where each of these criteria could be expressed as an individual query. In this section, let's see how we can make such a combination of search.

One simple way to express multiple search criteria is using a `bool` query. The `bool` query lets you use a combination of other queries, where each of the conditions can be put using a Boolean clause. There are three Boolean clauses:

- `must`

- `should`

- `must_not`

The `must` clause suggests that the constituent query must appear in the matching documents. If there is no `must` clause in the query, a combination of `should` clauses can be given. Also, you may set the minimum number of `should` clauses that should be matched. As the name indicates, `must_not` means that this clause should not match the document.

Let's see how we can use the `bool` query in Elasticsearch:

```
{
    "bool" : {
        "must" : [{
            "term" : { "productType" : "Laptop " }
        }],
        "must_not" : {
            "range" : {
                "dateOfManufactoring" :
                { "from" : 1990/01/01, "to" : 2014/01/01 }
            }
        },
        "should" : [
            {
                "term" : { "color" : "yellow" }
            },
            {
                "term" : { "description" : "lenovo" }
            }
        ],
        "minimum_should_match" : 1,
        "boost" : 1.0
    }
}
```

Here, we used a `bool` query to select all the laptops whose date of manufacturing is *not* between 1999 to 2014. Then, we boosted the laptops that were of the color yellow or were from lenovo.

If there is at least one `must` query, then none of the `should` queries need to match a document to qualify that document as a result. In this case, the `should` query match will increase the relevance of that document.

Sorting results

Sometimes, you may want to provide the user with a result set that is sorted based on a custom logic rather than the default scoring employed by Elasticsearch. Say you want to display some items that match your search query sorted according to the prize in the ascending or descending order. Elasticearch helps you do that quite easily. Let's see how various sort methods are used in Elasticsearch.

One thing that we should keep in mind while sorting is that the particular field based on which you sort, should be loaded in the memory. It's well and good if you have enough resources to sort. Sort is basically done on the field level. Elasticsearch provides support to perform sorting on arrays or multivalued fields.

However, if the sort field is an array or has multivalues, you can use any of the following functions to combine the result of these values in a single document to yield the sort value of that document:

- `min`
- `max`
- `sum`
- `avg`

As the name indicates, `min` picks the lowest value based on which sort is performed. Similarly, `max` sorts are based on the max value. If the `sum` mode is specified, the sum of all values is the basis of the sort. Similarly, `avg` takes the average value of all the values and performs the sort based on the average value.

Take a look at how sorting is done:

```
"query" : {
    ...
    },
    "sort" : [
        {"priceArray" : {"order" : "asc", "mode" : "avg"}}
    ]
}'
```

There is another sort option in Elasticsearch called as `_geo_distance`. It sorts the results based on their distance from a particular location. It would help you find nearest points — say if you are searching for restaurants near your location, you can get the results sorted according to the distance of each of the results from your location. Here is a sample code:

```
{
    "sort" : [
        {
            "_geo_distance" : {
                "pin.location" : [-70, 40],
                "order" : "asc",
                "unit" : "km"
            }
        }
    ],
    "query" : {
        "term" : { "type" : "restaurants" }
    }
}
```

There is yet another type of sorting that can done using scripts. We may seek the help of external scripts with which you can sort. This is a way of using a custom sorting technique if the default sort provided by Elasticsearch cannot fulfill your needs. The keyword `_script` denotes sorting with scripts. Look at this example:

```
{
    "query" : {
        ....
    },
    "sort" : {
        "_script" : {
            "script" : "doc['field_name'].value * factor",
            "type" : "number",
            "params" : {
                "factor" : 1.1
            },
            "order" : "asc"
        }
    }
}
```

By default, when using `sort`, the scores are ignored. If you want to track the score, you may use `track_scores` that should be set to `true`.

Using the scroll API for consistent pagination

Let's imagine this situation; first, the user queries for all laptops. The user receives 1,000 results and goes through the first page of 10 results. Now, some additional documents get added and in the background, instead of 1,000 matched results, we get 1,200 matched results. Hence, when the user opens the next page, they see some overlaps from the first page or mostly see some inconsistent results based on the score or aggregation. The number of Lenovo laptops that were shown on the first page were 20, but on the second page, this increased to 50.

This was because there were additional documents added between the time the first and second pages were served.

 The scroll API gives provision for a point-in-time search. New document addition/deletion won't be taken into account while using the Scroll API.

If you want to use the scroll API, you would need to specify the scroll parameter in the query string. This scroll parameter indicates Elasticsearch for how long it should keep the search context alive.

Take a look at this example:

```
curl -XGET 'localhost:9200/twitter/tweet/_search?scroll=1m' -d '
{
    "query": {
        "match" : {
            "title" : "Elasticsearch"
        }
    }
}
```

When the query is executed, we get a search result inclusive of scroll_id. It can be passed to the scroll API to get the next batch of results.

The scroll API can be used along with the scan type if you are not interested in the sort order:

```
curl 'localhost:9200/twitter/tweet/
  _search?scroll=1m&search_type=scan'  -d '
{
    "query": {
        "match" : {
```

```
                "title" : "Elasticsearch"
          }
       }
    }
```

In the preceding example, you would have noticed that we gave the time unit `1m` (one minute) with the search request. You would wonder if that is all that it takes to process the whole set of results. Definitely not. The time we give in the request is the time required to process the previous batch of results alone. Each call to the scroll API sets a new expiry time.

Autocomplete in Elasticsearch

Autocomplete provides suggestions while you type in a field. This feature is immensely helpful during search operations as it saves a user's time and also enables them to see various other related options in a single stretch. A `prefix` query is one way to implement this. A `prefix` query matches documents that have fields containing terms with the same prefix.

It is natural for you to think why we don't use a `prefix` query to solve the autocomplete problem or rather, what is the requirement for a separate API and module to implement autocomplete. The primary reason here is performance. The ideal data structure for autocomplete would be **finite state automata** (**FST**), which is explained in the following section, but then we are not storing tokens in FST in Lucene. Hence, it's only reasonable to maintain and have a separate module for autocomplete and to maintain a different data structure to store autocomplete-related data. It has to be noted that data related to autocomplete, is completely stored in the main memory.

How does FST help in faster autocompletes?

Let's assume that we are hosting an e-commerce website on network devices and we have the following products to offer:

- Copper plates
- Plain spoons
- Steel plates

Now, if someone enters the keyword `pla`, we should be able to display the complete words `copper plate` and `plain spoon`.

Internally, we store a data structure, as follows, to store this information:

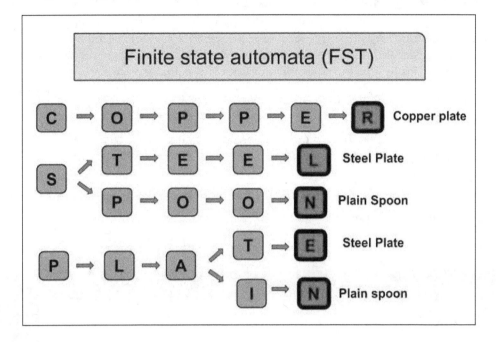

So, when a suggest request comes to Elasticsearch with the text `pla`, the possible paths to a final state (which is where the word ends) is the path `plate` and `plain`. On reaching the final state, the final state provides the actual text it stands for; in our case, `steel plate` and `plain spoon`. This flow of data can be easily understood from the following schematic:

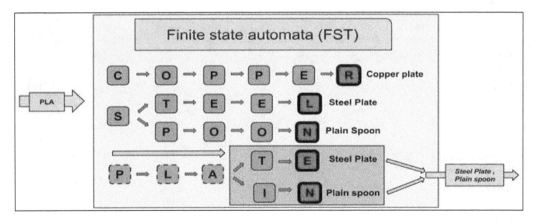

Hotel suggester using autocomplete

Let's take the scenario of a site like Zomato, which helps us to search hotels. As the first step, an autocomplete suggestion needs to be employed. When the user types, the autosuggester should be able to complete or give suggestions for the hotel names the end user tries to type in. The characteristics of this feature are as follows:

- It should be able to do a prefix match, that is a string such as `hot` should suggest `Hotel Holiday Inn` and `Hotel Summer Holiday Homes`.

- It should be able to map multiple prefixes, that is for a string `sum`, it should be able to suggest `Hotel Summer Holiday Homes`. Also, it should be case insensitive.

- It doesn't need index/type/ID information. It just needs the suggested text.

- It should be super fast.

An example of autocomplete is shown in the following figure for the word `chick`:

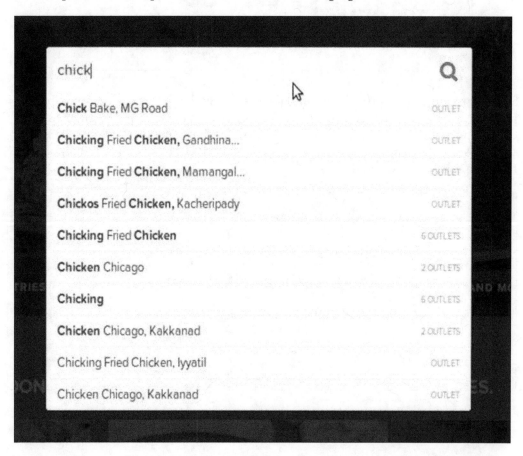

With this requirement in mind, let's see how we can implement this in Elasticsearch.

Elasticsearch offers you an out-of-the-box autocomplete feature. Remember that this feature is not implemented on the Lucene index and hence, none of the query or filters can be applied on it. Hence, we can make a context-independent auto suggest using Elasticsearch. For this purpose alone, Elasticsearch has a completion type associated with it. The completion type accepts multiple inputs and maps them to a single output. This is more like telling the suggester "Hey, if the user starts typing any of these words [chicken, chilli, tandoori], show him the output suggestion as Chicken chili tandoori."

Now, let's see how this is done. First, you need to specify in the mapping that we are dealing with an autocomplete field. So, the mapping for that type will look as follows:

```
curl -X PUT localhost:9200/restaurants/restaurant/_mapping -d '{
  "restaurant" : {
    "properties" : {
        "name" : { "type" : "string" },
        "restaurantSuggest" : { "type" : "completion",
                "index_analyzer" : "simple",
                "search_analyzer" : "simple",
                "payloads" : true
            }
        }
    }
}'
```

Here, first we defined a name field, which will hold the actual name of the restaurant and then the suggest field. We chose the suggest field named restaurantSuggest. A suggest field accepts *n* number of input strings and a single output string. This is to map multiple strings to a single output string. We can also specify a payload that usually has reference to the original document from where this suggest was generated. It's not mandatory to add this field. However, keeping in mind that the autosuggest doesn't give much contextual information from where it came from, it might be a good idea to add the document ID or something in the payload. Each document when indexed is given a unique ID called a document ID. We should provide this, or Elasticsearch would automatically assign a unique ID to it). In our case, we would include the document ID in the payload, so that we can go back and pick the original document in case the user selects that particular autocomplete suggestion:

```
curl -X PUT 'localhost:9200/restaurants/restaurant
  /royal-presidency-hotel' -d '{
    "name" : "Royal Presidency Hotel",
    "restaurantSuggest" : {
        "input": [ "Royal" ,  "Presidency" , "Hotel" ],
```

```
                "output": "Royal Presidency Hotel",
                "payload" : { "hotelID" : "royal-presidency-hotel" }
        }
    }'
    curl -X PUT 'localhost:9200/restaurants/restaurant
      /pan-indian-royal-restaurant' -d '{
        "name" : "Pan Indian Royal Restaurant",
        "restaurantSuggest" : {
            "input": [ "Pan" , "Indian" , "Royal" , "Restaurant" ],
            "output": "Pan Indian Royal Restaurant",
            "payload" : { "hotelID" : "pan-indian-royal-restaurant" }
        }
    }'
    curl -X PUT 'localhost:9200/restaurants/restaurant/
      chinese-dragon-restaurant' -d '{
        "name" : "Chinese Dragon restaurant",
        "restaurantSuggest" : {
            "input": [ "Chinese" , "Dragon" , "restaurant" ],
            "output": "Chinese Dragon restaurant",
            "payload" : { "hotelID" : "chinese-dragon-restaurant" }
        }
    }'
```

Here, as you can see, we indexed three documents on restaurants. Now, let's see how we can request a suggestion on uncompleted text input from the user:

```
curl -X POST 'localhost:9200/restaurants/_suggest?pretty' -d '{
    "restaurant-suggest" : {
        "text" : "roy",
        "completion" : {
            "field" : "restaurantSuggest"
        }
    }
}'
```

Here, we are requesting ES to autocomplete the text `roy` based on the `restaurantSuggest` field. The result is as follows:

```
{
  "_shards" : {
    "total" : 5,
    "successful" : 5,
    "failed" : 0
  },
  "restaurant-suggest" : [ {
    "text" : "roy",
```

```
      "offset" : 0,
      "length" : 3,
      "options" : [ {
        "text" : "Pan Indian Royal Restaurant",
        "score" : 1.0,
        "payload":{"hotelID":"pan-indian-royal-restaurant"}
      }, {
        "text" : "Royal Presidency Hotel",
        "score" : 1.0,
        "payload":{"hotelID":"royal-presidency-hotel"}
      } ]
    } ]
  }
```

We received two results and also the payload associated with it, which is the ID of the document from which it was generated. Note that the speed of this operation is much faster than the normal query requests. This is because of the FST storage structure we just used.

Summary

You learned various fitting pieces of an e-commerce application. You then learned how these can be realized in a much optimized manner using Elasticsearch. These are text search using a match query, a price or number range search using a range query, basic scoring methodologies, pagination, pagination with scroll for point in time pagination, clubbing various filters, and sorting.

We will look into scoring in detail in the next chapter. This topic has vast support from Elasticsearch and deserves a chapter of its own.

Relevancy and Scoring 3

As we are in the era of big data, it's very important that only the most relevant results are shown first. This means that even when there are millions of items that match our requirement, we only usually have the patience to go through the top limited number of items. For example, when we search for something in Google, it throws something like 234,324,000,000 results out of which, most of us would not even go to the second page. We usually constrain ourselves with the first page or the first 10 results. If the first 10 results are irrelevant, we assume that the next or remaining documents are more irrelevant than the current one and skip them too. This nature of Internet browsing has opened up huge scope for improvement in relevancy and scoring algorithms especially in the big data domain, as we have to deal with huge volumes of documents where mostly, only a few matter in their respective contexts.

The value scoring and relevancy give to an e-commerce site is invaluable. The core success of an e-commerce site depends on how many customers they can convert to buyers. One good strategy would be to learn the behavioral pattern of the users and to tempt them with products they are looking for. Geo location information can also be used to give them more meaningful results. Hence, an e-commerce business owes everything to a good relevancy algorithm that can show more meaningful results to the users and convert them to buyers.

Now, what constitutes a good scoring algorithm to find relevant or meaningful results? It can be many things. It can be how well the user's query matches a particular document. So in a news database, this would make a lot of sense. If a person searches for a cyclone in India, the news on cyclone and India would make more sense than news on the cyclone alone. In another context, results that are sorted based on geographical locations might make sense. For example, if I search for restaurants, then the restaurants near my locality would make more sense to me than the ones sitting half a globe away. There are also scenarios where I might want to learn the behavior of customers with respect to a set of products. I might want to throw random ordering of items and observe a pattern in which customers might favor an item in whatever order it's placed. In such cases, I might want to use a random ordering algorithm.

The support Elasticsearch provides you to score and for relevancy is simply way ahead of its time. You can score based on the statistic **term frequency–inverse document frequency (TF–IDF)**, a custom written script, filters, decay of numbers, dates, or even location and randomness. Even better, you can bring all these together to build a custom relevancy algorithm that fits your requirement.

How scoring works

Scoring is the process where we determine how well a query matches against a document. This can be based on the relevance of the query against the text it matches or based on a logic that we are interested in. For example, during a restaurant search on a site like Zomato, the closer the restaurant is, the better the match. In another instance, in a news search, a mix of recent news and a specific topic would give a better match.

[Scoring can be based on the query or on a custom logic.]

We will look at how custom logic can be introduced in scoring in the later part of this chapter. In this section, we will discuss how scoring is done on text based on the query text.

There are three main factors that determine the score of a query against a text field, which are as follows:

1. **Term frequency**: Let's assume that we are searching for the word `elephant`, we get the following results:

    ° **Document-1**: `There are two types of elephants, African elephant and Indian elephant.`

    ° **Document-2**: `Elephants, cow and dogs roamed around the streets.`

    Which would be a better match? Obviously, Document-1 would be a better match. This is attributed to the fact that the word elephant has more occurrences in Document-1 than Document-2. What this actually means is that the word elephant is more important in Document-1 than Document-2.

2. **Inverse document frequency**: Let's say, we have a database of books. There can be various book titles in it. Now, if I search for `Java book`, would it make sense if I treat the token `java` and `book` equally? Most probably not because `java` is very much centric to our search, but the token `book` is less important, as it would be very common throughout the index.

   Let's take another example:

   - ○ **Document-1**: `Python book by Packt`
   - ○ **Document-2**: `Java by Packt`
   - ○ **Document-3**: `Ruby book`

   Let's say, I am searching for the string `Java book`. Now, the token `java` is there in Document-2 and the token `book` is present in Document-1. Will it make sense to give equal weight to Document-1 and Document-2? Well, of course not. This is because `book` is a very common token throughout the index and it doesn't make sense to treat the token `java` and `book` the same. Hence, we use a mathematical model to compute this differentiating factor. It is called as the **inverse document frequency (IDF)**.

   IDF computes how common a token is and decreases its weighting during a search. Hence, rare terms get more preference over common terms.

3. **Field length**: Field length of the document string also counts for a lot. It would be safe to assume that the shorter the string, the better the match.

   Let's take a look at an example:

   - ○ **Document-1**: `Facebook is one of the best social media websites`
   - ○ **Document-2**: `Facebook , Orkut , G+ are some of the best social media websites`

   When we search for the term `facebook`, which of these documents are a better match? Document-1 would be a better match. This is attributed from the fact that the lesser the field length, the more we can assume that the matched term has a better relevancy for that document.

The default score computed per document for a query is a function of term frequency, inverse document frequency, and field length normalization.

How to debug scoring

When we get results for our query, we usually get the matched document and its computed score. This score defines the degree of match between the query and that document. As explained before, this value can be computed using the TF-IDF algorithm or using some custom score based on a user's requirement. In many situations, we need to understand how this value was computed or the entire scoring process might look like a black box. In such cases, the **explain** flag comes to our rescue.

 For any search query, you can enable the explain flag to see how the score is computed.

Enabling the explain flag gives us a neat JSON file per document briefly explaining the different functions used to compute a score, its input values, and output. Finally, it briefly explains how they are combined to serve the final score or result.

To enable the flag, apply the following query:

```
curl -XPOST 'http://localhost:9200/medicalrecords/medicalrecord/
_search?pretty' -d '{
  "explain": true,
  "query": {
    "match": {
      "content": "red"
    }
  }
}'
```

The result of the preceding query is as follows:

```
{
  "took" : 2,
  "timed_out" : false,
  "_shards" : {
    "total" : 1,
    "successful" : 1,
    "failed" : 0
  },
  "hits" : {
    "total" : 1,
    "max_score" : 0.3709857,
    "hits" : [ {
      "_shard" : 0,
      "_node" : "QKlMXoNsRIqAVPOo5sk6VA",
      "_index" : "medicalrecords",
```

The node value and the shard value from which this document came. This value is otherwise not available if we don't use the explain flag.

```
"_type" : "medicalrecord",
"_id" : "QsdkLpyKSqGh-7hzhtjfvA",
"_score" : 0.3709857,
"_source":{  "title": "Nausea and vomiting hits bad",
"content": "Initial symptoms includes red eyes , nausea ,
vomiting ,red eyes , chest pain and cough. Later blood from
eyes and bruises was noticed. Chest pain and coughing was
also noticed.At a latest stage , bleeding from other
orifices like mouth , nose are also noticed. The patient is
in a really bad critical condition now.", "date": "2014-10-
01 03:02:05", "peopleWithSimilarSymptoms": 1,
"PatientPastHealthIndex" : 6,   "LocationPastHealthIndex" :
2, "location": { "lat": "2.224", "lon": "2.335" }},
"_explanation" : {
  "value" : 0.37098572,
  "description" : "weight(content:red in 3)
  [PerFieldSimilarity], result of:",
```

The following shows how the score from term frequency, inverse document frequency, and field normalization is combined.

```
"details" : [ {
  "value" : 0.37098572,
  "description" : "score(doc=3,freq=2.0 =
  termFreq=2.0\n), product of:",
```

Inverse document frequency computation:

```
"details" : [
{
  "value" : 0.99999994,
  "description" : "queryWeight, product of:",
  "details" : [ {
    "value" : 2.0986123,
    "description" : "idf(docFreq=1, maxDocs=6)"
  }, {
    "value" : 0.47650534,
    "description" : "queryNorm"
  } ]
},
{
  "value" : 0.37098575,
  "description" : "fieldWeight in 3, product of:",
  "details" : [ {
```

```
          "value" : 1.4142135,
          "description" : "tf(freq=2.0), with freq of:",
          "details" : [ {
            "value" : 2.0,
            "description" : "termFreq=2.0"
```

Term frequency computation:

```
          } ]
        },
        {
          "value" : 2.0986123,
          "description" : "idf(docFreq=1, maxDocs=6)"
        }, {
          "value" : 0.125,
          "description" : "fieldNorm(doc=3)"
```

Field normalization computation:

```
          } ]
        } ]
      } ]
    }
  } ]
 }
}
```

The Ebola outbreak

In 2014, the world witnessed the outbreak of a dangerous epidemic called Ebola. When the Ebola outbreak first started, scientists all over the world started studying the disease. They were not very sure about the disease name nor what it was named, but they were aware that a disease has appeared and they also knew some of its symptoms. A biotechnology scientist in America wanted to learn about the outbreak of this disease and wanted to learn its patterns. For that reason, he obtained the medical records from various African hospitals where the disease was reported. He knew the symptoms of this new born disease and wanted to see the medical records in order to find the records that most probably contained the symptoms of the disease, which we now know as Ebola.

A medical record from the hospitals had the following information:

- **Title**: An unstructured single line of text giving the title of the description.

- **Description**: A detailed analysis of the disease, symptoms, patient, medicines tried, and the patient's current condition. This field is also unstructured, but it's guaranteed that this field captures the symptoms of the disease very well.

- **PatientPastHealthIndex**: This is a structured field. It gives an index that is between 1 and 10. This number signifies the past health status of the patient. If the patient was very healthy in the past and had made fewer visits to the hospital, then he will get a 10. If the patient was very unhealthy, was diagnosed with disease in the past, and also has been admitted a number of times, then his index would be 1. The presence of sugar, cholesterol, and other unhealthy supplementary diseases is also taken into account while making this index.

- **LocationPastHealthIndex**: This signifies an index that represents how healthy an area is. If it's an area that is reported with lots of diseases and a larger volume of people showing up in hospitals, the index would be 1. If it's a very healthy location with fewer people showing up in the hospitals, then the index is 10.

- **PatientsWithSimilarSymptom**: This number signifies the number of patients in an hospital who have reported similar symptoms.

- **Date**: This is the date on which this patient's illness was reported.

- **Location**: This represents the latitude and longitude of the hospital.

The scientist wanted to try out various sorting mechanisms for the documents and see which scheme would fit well. The following are the various schemes that came into his mind to help him to sort the records in a way that the records with a bigger probability of having the new disease appear first.

Boost match in the title field column over description

The problem: The scientist noticed that the symptoms that appeared more predominantly were marked in the title and the less predominant ones were included in the description. Hence, when he searched for symptoms, he wanted to search for the terms both in the title and description. Also, he believed that the match on the title should be given more preference over a match in the description.

How to solve it: This can be solved using a match query or the function score query. However, the quickest and easiest way to do this would be to use the `multi_match` query. We can run the match query over multiple fields and give the match preference for each field:

Query:

```
{
    "query": {
      "multi_match": {
        "fields": [
          "title^10",
```

In the preceding code, we boosted the importance of the `title` field by giving it 10 times more priority over the content field by giving it a `^10` expression:

```
          "content"
        ],
        "query": "nausea"
      }
    }
}
```

Response:

```
{
    "took": 2,
    "timed_out": false,
    "_shards": {
      "total": 1,
      "successful": 1,
      "failed": 0
    },
    "hits": {
      "total": 4,
      "max_score": 0.5633609,
      "hits": [
        {
          "_index": "medicalrecords",
          "_type": "medicalrecord",
          "_id": "uJdI7zsOQrC91A5DQtkAKA",
          "_score": 0.5633609,
          "_source": {
```

As `nausea` came in both the title and content fields, this document came in first:

```
    "title": "Nausea and vomiting hits bad",
    "content": "Initial symptoms includes red eyes , nausea
    , vomiting ,red eyes , chest pain and cough. Later blood
    from eyes and bruises was noticed. Chest pain and
    coughing was also noticed.At a latest stage , bleeding
    from other orifices like mouth , nose are also noticed.
    The patient is in a really bad critical condition now.",
    "date": "2014-10-01 03:02:05",
    "peopleWithSimilarSymptoms": 1,
    "PatientPastHealthIndex": 6,
    "LocationPastHealthIndex": 2,
    "location": {
      "lat": "2.2222",
      "lon": "2.332"
    }
  }
},
{
  "_index": "medicalrecords",
  "_type": "medicalrecord",
  "_id": "JTFGAya_SL-zNWDDCD7RDg",
  "_score": 0.40240064,
  "_source": {
```

Though the occurrence of `nausea` comes in the first document, as the length of the title field is larger, more relevance is computed for the first document:

```
    "title": "Patient with nausea and head ache followed by
    cough",
    "content": "A patient was reported with rash initially
    then nausea.Vomiting and headache was followed.He was
    advised to rest",
    "date": "2014-02-01 02:01:01",
    "peopleWithSimilarSymptoms": 1,
    "PatientPastHealthIndex": 3,
    "LocationPastHealthIndex": 4,
    "location": {
      "lat": "2.2222",
      "lon": "2.332"
    }
  }
},
{
  "_index": "medicalrecords",
```

```
      "_type": "medicalrecord",
      "_id": "OIFCQKSaTxextf7a4eAvzQ",
      "_score": 0.01698789,
      "_source": {
```

As the token Nausea is not present in the title field, this document is made less relevant:

```
        "title": "Unidentified disease symptoms in Tanzania",
        "content": "The patient is having a bad fever , nausea
        and vomiting. This was followed by chest pain , raised
        rash.",
        "date": "2014-11-01 01:01:02",
        "peopleWithSimilarSymptoms": 2,
        "PatientPastHealthIndex": 9,
        "LocationPastHealthIndex": 4,
        "location": {
          "lat": "2.2212",
          "lon": "2.312"
        }
      }
    },
    {
      "_index": "medicalrecords",
      "_type": "medicalrecord",
      "_id": "eoc4QygWTPudNxYkBgMnUw",
      "_score": 0.009707365,
      "_source": {
        "title": "Fever like disease found. Cure not working",
        "content": "It started with a bad fever , nausea and
        vomiting. This was followed by chest pain , raised rash.
        None of the medicines for fever or rash is not to be
        taking any effect.Later it was also observed that there
        was bleeding from the eyes",
        "date": "2014-11-01 05:01:01",
        "peopleWithSimilarSymptoms": 7,
        "PatientPastHealthIndex": 3,
        "LocationPastHealthIndex": 9,
        "location": {
          "lat": "2.2222",
          "lon": "2.332"
        }
      }
    }
  ]
}
```

Most recently published medical journals

The problem: To start his work, the scientist felt that an option to view the most recent medical journals would help him evaluate the current situation. Hence, he wanted to search for certain terms such as nausea, vomiting, and so on, which are more like the symptoms of Ebola, and see the latest journals that had any of these terms.

How to solve this: The `function` query would be the best fit for this. We can mention the query in the query section and then use the field function to mark the date field as a scoring mechanism. Later, we can replace the score given by our query with the score given by the date function so that the order of documents returned is based on how recent the medical journals are.

The following code snippet is used to make a request:

```
{
    "query": {
      "function_score": {
        "query": {
          "multi_match": {
            "fields": [
              "title",
              "content"
            ],
            "query": "nausea"
          }
        },
        "functions": [
          {
```

Include the value of date as a score:

```
            "field_value_factor": {
              "field": "date"
            }
          }
        ],
```

Replace the score generated with the query with the one computed by our function:

```
        "boost_mode": "replace"
      }
    }
}
```

The following is the response to the preceding request:

Score	Time	Title
1.41481804E12	2014-11-01 05:01:01	Fever-like disease found. The cure is not working.
1.41480362E12	2014-11-01 01:01:02	Unidentified disease symptoms in Tanzania.
1.4121325E12	2014-10-01 03:02:05	Nausea and vomiting hits bad.
1.3912201E12	2014-02-01 02:01:01	Patient with Nausea and headache followed by cough.

The most recent Ebola report on healthy patients

The problem: Next, the scientist felt that he needed the most recent document and the one with the highest probability of being an Ebola case. He felt that Ebola was a deadly disease and it can infect even a healthy person. So, if a person who has a high health index is affected by a disease, he still wanted to inspect that person's medical record. He also wanted the most recent of such documents, but recency should not supersede the idea of a healthy person getting infected and be given more priority.

How to solve it: Here, as we need the notion of recency in the sorting scheme, we sort the medical journals based on the day and not on the entire timestamp. This means that a medical journal that was published on 21st will have more priority over a medical journal that was published on 20th. However, no two medical journals from the same day will have the same priorities. For the same day, if we can sort the journals based on PersonHealthIndex, this will bring the concept of healthy people getting affected into the equation. So, by joining these two, we can bring both a notion of recency and the concept of healthy people becoming infected to the ordering of records. We also can use the function query for this purpose. We will use the script function to extract the date (and not time) information from the date field. We can then use the field function to extract PersonHealthIndex. Now, summing up or multiplying these two values might not give you an accurate value of the overall score. This is because the timestamp value is way higher than PersonHealthIndex. So, a better idea would be to multiply the timestamp epoch value by 10, which is the range of PersonHealthIndex and then add it to PersonHealthIndex. For this, we can use the add boostType parameter of the function query.

The request:

```
{
  "query": {
    "function_score": {
      "query": {
        "multi_match": {
```

```
        "fields": [
          "title",
          "content"
        ],
        "query": "nausea vomiting red eyes"
      }
    },
    "functions": [
      {
        "script_score": {
```

We use the script score function for a score that signifies the day of the year. We need to take out the hour/minute/second perception out of it. So, we multiply the epoch by a day worth of time and get a score that only measures the time of the day:

```
        "script": "doc['date'].value/(1000*60*60*24)"
      }
    },
    {
```

Next, we need to compute a score signifying the patient's past health:

```
      "field_value_factor": {
        "field": "PatientPastHealthIndex"
      }
    }
  ],
```

Then, we compute the score given by each function:

```
  "score_mode": "sum",
```

We replace the score from functions with the score given by the query:

```
  "boost_mode": "replace"
      }
    }
  }
```

The response:

_Score	Date	PatientPastHealthIndex	Title
16384.0	2014-11-01 01:01:02	9	Unidentified disease symptoms in Tanzania.
16378.0	2014-11-01 05:01:01	3	Fever-like disease found. The cure does not work.
16350.	2014-10-01 03:02:05	6	Nausea and vomiting hits bad.
16105.0	2014-02-01 02:01:01	3	Patient with Nausea and headache followed by cough.

Boosting certain symptoms over others

The problem: It had become very clear that there was another disease that had similar symptoms to Ebola. This disease was misunderstood or wrongly diagnosed as Ebola. The scientist found the differentiating symptoms of this wrongly diagnosed disease and wanted to give a negative boost to these symptoms alone. He also wanted to boost those symptoms that had a better probability of being diagnosed as Ebola. Hence, he came up with a set of symptoms that he wanted to boost and another set of symptoms that he wanted to negatively boost.

How to solve it: The best query candidate would be a boost query. In a boost query, we can assign a set of queries whose boost values are given a positive boost and another set of queries, whose boost values are given a negative boost. Hence, a match query on title and description of positive symptoms in the positive section and a match query on title and description of negative symptoms in the negative section should do the trick.

The request:

```
{
  "query": {
    "boosting": {
      "positive": {
        "multi_match": {
          "fields": [
            "title",
            "content"
          ],
```

We boost the words nausea and fever positively because they are strong symptoms:

```
          "query": "nausea fever"
        }
      },
      "negative": {
        "multi_match": {
          "fields": [
            "title",
            "content"
          ],
```

We negatively boost the words headache and cough as these symptoms might suggest that it's not Ebola but some other disease:

```
          "query": "headache cough"
        }
      },
```

Apply a negative boost of 2, this is a mandatory field:

```
        "negative_boost": 2
      }
    }
  }
```

The response for the preceding code is as follows:

```
{
  "took": 6,
  "timed_out": false,
  "_shards": {
    "total": 1,
    "successful": 1,
    "failed": 0
  },
  "hits": {
    "total": 4,
    "max_score": 0.3410297,
    "hits": [
      {
        "_index": "medicalrecords",
        "_type": "medicalrecord",
        "_id": "uJdI7zsOQrC91A5DQtkAKA",
        "_score": 0.3410297,
        "_source": {
          "title": "Nausea and vomiting hits bad",
```

The negative symptoms are not present and we have lots of positive symptoms:

```
          "content": "Initial symptoms includes red eyes , nausea
          , vomiting ,red eyes , chest pain and cough. Later
          blood from eyes and bruises was noticed. Chest pain and
          coughing was also noticed.At a latest stage , bleeding
          from other orifices like mouth , nose are also noticed.
          The patient is in a really bad critical condition
          now.",
          "date": "2014-10-01 03:02:05",
          "peopleWithSimilarSymptoms": 1,
          "PatientPastHealthIndex": 6,
          "LocationPastHealthIndex": 2,
          "location": {
            "lat": "2.2222",
            "lon": "2.332"
          }
```

```
        }
    },
    {
        "_index": "medicalrecords",
        "_type": "medicalrecord",
        "_id": "OIFCQKSaTxextf7a4eAvzQ",
        "_score": 0.27335078,
        "_source": {
            "title": "Unidentified disease symptoms in Tanzania",
            "content": "The patient is having a bad fever , nausea
            and vomiting. This was followed by chest pain , raised
            rash.",
            "date": "2014-11-01 01:01:02",
            "peopleWithSimilarSymptoms": 2,
            "PatientPastHealthIndex": 9,
            "LocationPastHealthIndex": 4,
            "location": {
                "lat": "2.2212",
                "lon": "2.312"
            }
        }
    },
    {
        "_index": "medicalrecords",
        "_type": "medicalrecord",
        "_id": "eoc4QygWTPudNxYkBgMnUw",
        "_score": 0.25268972,
        "_source": {
            "title": "Fever like disease found. Cure not working",
            "content": "It started with a bad fever , nausea  and
            vomiting. This was followed by chest pain , raised rash.
            None of the medicines for fever or rash is not to be
            taking any effect.Later it was also observed that there
            was bleeding from the eyes",
            "date": "2014-11-01 05:01:01",
            "peopleWithSimilarSymptoms": 7,
            "PatientPastHealthIndex": 3,
            "LocationPastHealthIndex": 9,
            "location": {
                "lat": "2.2222",
                "lon": "2.332"
            }
        }
    },
    {
```

```
  "_index": "medicalrecords",
  "_type": "medicalrecord",
  "_id": "JTFGAya_SL-zNWDDCD7RDg",
  "_score": 0.24359263,
  "_source": {
    "title": "Patient with Nausea and head ache followed by
    cough",
```

Lots of negative symptoms and hence, the least score. Let's take a look at the following code snippet:

```
"content": "A patient was reported with rash initially
then nausea. Vomiting and headache was followed. He was
advised to rest",
"date": "2014-02-01 02:01:01",
"peopleWithSimilarSymptoms": 1,
"PatientPastHealthIndex": 3,
"LocationPastHealthIndex": 4,
"location": {
  "lat": "2.2222",
  "lon": "2.332"
}
        }
      }
    ]
  }
}
```

Random ordering of medical journals for different interns

The problem: Seeing that there were a large volume of medical records, the scientist appointed a set of interns from a reputed medical college to study the records. He didn't want to do any particular scoring as he feared that this might lead to biased results or add prejudice to the interns' judgment. On searching the journals and once the top results were shown, he wanted to see the pattern in which the interns opened the medical journals that they felt were more suspicious. As there is no specific order to do this, these interns went through the titles of all the journals and chose to open certain journals for further study. The scientist felt that the documents that were studied this way could be more important for his study. Hence, he wanted to show a different order of documents for different interns. This means that if an intern searched based on some keywords, the ordering of the results wouldn't be the same for a different intern who also searched based on the same set of keywords. Hence, the scientist wanted different ordering of results for each search so that he could learn the study pattern of the interns.

How to solve it: The random function provided in the function score query would be the best fit for this. This function generates a random score every time it's used. Hence for each search hit, a totally different order is taken as a score. We will multiply the query score of a document with this value so that the search query has some influence on the order of results. We respect the close matches of a query toward a document, but also maintain randomness.

The request:

```
{
  "query": {
    "function_score": {
      "query": {
        "multi_match": {
          "fields": [
            "title",
            "content"
          ],
          "query": "nausea vomiting red eyes"
        }
      },
      "functions": [
        {
```

This request computes random score. Hence, we can achieve a different order in each request:

```
          "random_score": {}
        }
      ],
      "boost_mode": "multiply"
```

We multiply this random score with the score computed by the query so that the query has a minimal influence on the ordering of results:

```
    }
}
```

The response:

The response of this query would be different for each query. So, we can observe slightly different orders for different queries:

Document order	The first request	The second request	The third request	The fourth request
#1	DocumentA	DocumentD	DocumentB	DocumentA
#2	DocumentC	DocumentC	DocumentD	DocumentC
#3	DocumentB	DocumentB	DocumentC	DocumentB
#4	DocumentD	DocumentA	DocumentA	DocumentD

Medical journals from the closest place to the Ebola outbreak

The problem: By sorting the medical journals based on a date and inspecting the density of patients who reported Ebola, the scientist could accurately find the area from where Ebola originated. He did a search on medical journals that had mentioned the symptoms of Ebola and arranged them based on a date. The area from where Ebola was reported initially was thus found. Now, the scientist felt that the patients affected by Ebola for the longest period of time could be found here. If such patients could be found, he could study the prolonged effect of Ebola and the average time until their death. So now, he wanted to search medical journals closest to a particular place and the journals that had probable symptoms of Ebola, which will infect the patients eventually. The eventual symptoms are bleeding of nose, mouth, and other orifices.

How to solve it: Even here, our friendly function query comes to the rescue. We can use the query part to filter the journals that have Ebola symptoms and then, we can use the decay function on location to decide the ordering.

The query:

```
{
  "query": {
    "function_score": {
      "query": {
        "multi_match": {
          "fields": [
            "title",
            "content"
```

```
      ],
      "query": "nausea vomiting red eyes"
    }
  },
  "functions": [
    {
      "linear": {
        "location": {
          "scale": "1km",
          Ebola was first reported here
          "origin": {
            "lat": "2.2212",
            "lon": "2.312"
          }
        }
      }
    }
  ],
  "boost_mode": "replace"
    }
  }
}
```

The response:

_score	Geo location	Title
0.9150084	2.226,2.319	Unidentified disease symptoms in Tanzania.
0.7876279	2.2242,2.333	Patient with nausea and headache followed by cough.
0.7828477	2.227,2.3329	Fever-like disease found. The cure does not work.
0.7680406	2.224,2.335	Nausea and vomiting hits bad.

Medical journals from unhealthy places near the Ebola outbreak

The problem: The scientist now wanted to see the effect of Ebola on the already certified unhealthy places due to their poor medical history. He felt that any distance of 10 km around the Ebola outbreak should be considered with equal relevance. Any distance beyond that should have lesser relevance in the order of distance. That is, the longer the distance from the Ebola outbreak, the lesser the relevance. Now, medical records from the hospital that reported poor history of health should be given a greater relevance.

How to solve it: The function score query would be the best candidate to solve this. We will weave two functions for each relevancy scoring logic and combine them using the multiplication operation. Now, this score would be replaced with the score generated by the query to achieve the functionality. To implement the logic of relevance due to distance, we can use the decay function over the location field. There is an offset attribute in the decay function that controls the point from where relevance calculation starts the decay. We can set this to 10 km. Another decay function on LocationHealthIndex can be used to enumerate the second relevance logic.

The request:

```
{
  "query": {
    "function_score": {
      "query": {
        "multi_match": {
          "fields": [
            "title",
            "content"
          ],
          "query": "nausea vomiting red eyes"
        }
      },
      "functions": [
        {
          "linear": {
            "location": {
              "scale": "1km",
              "offset": "10km",
              "origin": {
                "lat": "2.2212",
                "lon": "2.312"
              }
            }
          }
        },
        {
          "gauss": {
            "LocationPastHealthIndex": {
              "origin": 0,
              "scale": 1
            }
          }
        }
```

```
        ],
        "boost_mode": "replace"
      }
    }
  }
```

The response:

Score	Location	Location health index	Title
0.057570856	2.224,2.335	2	Nausea and vomiting hits bad.
1.5258789E-5	2.226,2.319	4	Unidentified disease symptoms in Tanzania.
1.4221428E-5	2.2242,2.333	4	Patient with Nausea and headache followed by cough.
3.843742E-25	2.227,2.3329	9	Fever-like disease found. Cure does not work.

Healthy people from unhealthy locations have Ebola symptoms

The problem: Based on various medical indices provided in the medical journals, namely Location, Person, and SimilarDiseaseReported, the scientist found a formula that could better predict the change of Ebola infection in the medical journal. He formulated a complex mathematical formula based on these three parameters. The equation for the same is as follows:

$$\_score = PatientPastHealthIndex + 10 / LocationPastHealthIndex$$

How to solve it: In the function score query, we use the script function type to compute the preceding formula.

The request:

```
{
  "query": {
    "function_score": {
      "query": {
        "multi_match": {
          "fields": [
            "title",
            "content"
          ],
```

```
        "query": "nausea vomiting red eyes"
      }
    },
    "functions": [
      {
        "script_score": {
          "script": "doc['PatientPastHealthIndex'].value +
          10/doc['LocationPastHealthIndex'].value"
        }
      }
    ],
    "boost_mode": "replace"
  }
 }
}
```

The response:

Score	Patient Health Index	Location Health Index	Title
11	9	4	Unidentified disease symptoms in Tanzania.
11	6	2	Nausea and vomiting hits bad.
5	3	4	Patient with Nausea and headache followed by cough.
4	3	9	Fever-like disease found. Cure does not work.

Relevancy based on the order in which the symptoms appeared

The problem: The order in which the symptoms appeared was observed to be a major indication of Ebola. It was observed that nausea and then rash, in that order, were the indicators and the scientist wanted to arrange the results in this order.

The script:

```
nauseaPos = -1;
if(_index['content'].get('nausea',_POSITIONS).tf() > 0){
  nauseaPos =
  _index['content'].get('nausea',_POSITIONS)[0].position;
}
rashPos = -1;
if(_index['content'].get('rash',_POSITIONS).tf() > 0){
```

```
    rashPos = _index['content'].get('rash',_POSITIONS)[0].position;
  }
overallScore = -1;
if(nauseaPos > -1 && rashPos > -1 && nauseaPos < rashPos){
  overallScore = 1
}
return overallScore;
```

How to solve it: In the script, put the following code:

```
Request - {
  "query": {
    "function_score": {
      "query": {
        "multi_match": {
          "fields": [
            "title",
            "content"
          ],
          "query": "nausea vomiting red eyes"
        }
      },
      "functions": [
        {
          "script_score": {
            "script": "getScore"
          }
        }
      ],
      "boost_mode": "replace"
    }
  }
}
```

The response:

```
"hits": [
  {
    "_index": "medicalrecords",
    "_type": "medicalrecord",
    "_id": "OIFCQKSaTxextf7a4eAvzQ",
    "_score": 1.0,
    "_source": {
```

Nausea is followed by a rash here, hence the higher score:

```
"title": "Unidentified disease symptoms in Tanzania",
"content": "The patient is having a bad fever , nausea
and vomiting. This was followed by chest pain , raised
rash.",
"date": "2014-11-01 01:01:02",
"peopleWithSimilarSymptoms": 2,
"PatientPastHealthIndex": 9,
"LocationPastHealthIndex": 4,
"location": {
  "lat": "2.2212",
  "lon": "2.312"
}
}
},
{
  "_index": "medicalrecords",
  "_type": "medicalrecord",
  "_id": "eoc4QygWTPudNxYkBgMnUw",
  "_score": 1.0,
  "_source": {
    "title": "Fever like disease found. Cure not working",
    "content": "It started with a bad fever , nausea  and
vomiting. This was followed by chest pain , raised rash.
None of the medicines for fever or rash is not to be
taking any effect.Later it was also observed that there
was bleeding from the eyes",
    "date": "2014-11-01 05:01:01",
    "peopleWithSimilarSymptoms": 7,
    "PatientPastHealthIndex": 3,
    "LocationPastHealthIndex": 9,
    "location": {
      "lat": "2.2222",
      "lon": "2.332"
    }
  }
},
{
  "_index": "medicalrecords",
  "_type": "medicalrecord",
  "_id": "uJdI7zsOQrC91A5DQtkAKA",
  "_score": -1.0,
  "_source": {
```

```
      "title": "Nausea and vomiting hits bad",
      "content": "Initial symptoms includes red eyes , nausea
      , vomiting ,red eyes , chest pain and cough. Later blood
      from eyes and bruises was noticed. Chest pain and
      coughing was also noticed.At a latest stage , bleeding
      from other orifices like mouth , nose are also noticed.
      The patient is in a really bad critical condition now.",
      "date": "2014-10-01 03:02:05",
      "peopleWithSimilarSymptoms": 1,
      "PatientPastHealthIndex": 6,
      "LocationPastHealthIndex": 2,
      "location": {
        "lat": "2.2222",
        "lon": "2.332"
      }
    }
  },
  {
    "_index": "medicalrecords",
    "_type": "medicalrecord",
    "_id": "JTFGAya_SL-zNWDDCD7RDg",
    "_score": -1.0,
    "_source": {
      "title": "Patient with Nausea and head ache followed by
      cough",
      "content": "A patient was reported with rash initially
      then nausea.Vomiting and headache was followed. He was
      advised to rest",
      "date": "2014-02-01 02:01:01",
      "peopleWithSimilarSymptoms": 1,
      "PatientPastHealthIndex": 3,
      "LocationPastHealthIndex": 4,
      "location": {
        "lat": "2.2222",
        "lon": "2.332"
      }
    }
  }
]
```

Summary

You understood the power and flexibility of Elasticsearch to implement your own scoring logic in this chapter. This flexibility can be utilized for a variety of purposes, mainly in the e-commerce industry. A lot of intellectual properties can be built over this platform, which would be the core of many business logics.

Let's do a recap on how scoring can be done. It can be divided as follows:

- **A query-based score**: This is the score returned by Elasticsearch on the text match. This is computed based on term frequency, inverse document frequency, and field length normalization. Under this section, you learned that you can also do the following:
    - ° You can boost a match on certain fields over others using the multi field option in the match query
    - ° You can boost certain queries over others in the bool query

- **Custom score based on user requirements**: Using the function query, we can implement various functions that provide scores on their own. Later, the scores that are returned by various functions can be brought together to get the final score emitted by the custom score functions. These functions are:
    - ° **Score based on a filter**: This is a compute score based on a filter. If the filter matches, you need to emit the score value as X.
    - ° **Score based on the decay of numeric values**: Provided there is a reference point, the closer the numerical value, the better the score. Here, the user has to give a reference point. The greater the distance from the reference point, the lesser the relevancy. The numerical value can be a geo point, date, number, or even an IP.

- **Score based on a random value**: Here, a score is computed randomly for different calls.

Finally, in the function query, we have options to club the scores returned by these two scoring logics.

In the next chapter, we will see how we can use the document linking or relational features of Elasticsearch. However, you need to remember that it's very hard to implement relational documents in a distributed network. Most of the NoSQL solutions don't have an option for this, but then Elasticsearch has a substantial feature set that can support this to a great extent.

4
Managing Relational Content

Representing real-world data is very decisive in the sense that usually, straight data structures won't always suffice for your needs. Often, you would find yourself in a position where you would need to adopt a complex structure for your data with some kind of a relation within objects. Here, in this chapter, we will see how Elasticsearch provides provisions to manage such relational content. Here are the topics that we will cover in this chapter:

- Parent-child search
- Limitations on a query on nested fields
- Solution 1 – nested datatype
- Solution 2– parent-child datatype
- Schema design to store questions and answers
- Searching questions based on a criteria of answers
- Searching answers based on a criteria of questions
- Term lookup

Elasticsearch provides a number of ways with which you can manage relational content. Of those, the simplest way is to directly add inner objects within your structure. Let's see how simple inner objects in Elasticsearch behave.

The product-with-tags search problem

A new requirement came into existence to search for products that have a specific attribute value set.

As in, the user should be able to search for a particular product based on any of its attributes. However, these attributes are not fixed and might change on a daily basis. Hence, it's not possible to keep this as a key-value pair. More keys mean more fields and each field costs Lucene a reverse index under the hood. So, a better approach would be to model the data as follows:

```
/products/product/LCD_TV

    {
      "name" : "LCD TV",
      "tags" : [
        {
          "tagName" : "company" ,
          "value" : "Sony"
        },
        {
          "tagName" : "competitor" ,
          "value" : "Toshiba"
        }
      ]
    }
```

With this approach, everything looks good, but then, the following query works true for the preceding document:

```
tags.tagName:company AND tags.value:Toshiba
```

This is not what we expected. The product actually belongs to the company Sony, but then, it matched against the company Toshiba.

Here, a closer look at the approach makes us realize that this issue stems from the reverse index data structure. What happens is, in the reverse index, for each field, each token is mapped against its document IDs.

Hence the tags are stored internally as follows:

```
Tags.tagName => [ "company" , "competitor]
Tags.value => [ "sony" , "Toshiba" ]
```

That is why the AND operation on both the conditions is successful, but logically, it doesn't suit us. This issue is referred to as flattening of documents.

Nested types to the rescue

Using the nested datatype is one alternative for the inner objects and it solves the issue with the flattening of documents in Elasticsearch. Let's see how we can use the nested datatype. Let's consider the following example:

```
curl -XPOST localhost:9200/authors/author/1 -d'{
  "name": "Multi G. Enre",
  "books": [
    {
      "name": "Guns and lasers",
      "genre": "scifi",
      "publisher": "orbit"
    },
    {
      "name": "Dead in the night",
      "genre": "thriller",
      "publisher": "penguin"
    }
  ]
}'
curl -XPOST localhost:9200/authors/author/2 -d'{
  "name": "Alastair Reynolds",
  "books": [
    {
      "name": "Revelation Space",
      "genre": "scifi",
      "publisher": "penguin"
    }
  ]
}'
```

If you examine carefully, you would ideally notice no difference as to how the document looks like when compared to the inner objects. This is true as well. To make your Elasticsearch instance understand your intention of using the nested datatype, you must mention the mapping explicitly as a nested one. Take a look at how this is done:

```
curl -XPOST localhost:9200/authors/nested_author/_mapping -d '{
  "nested_author":{
    "properties":{
      "books": {
        "type": "nested"
      }
    }
  }
}'
```

In the preceding code, we mentioned the books as a nested datatype. Once this mapping is specified, Elasticsearch deals with the nested structure internally. This enables the queries that were unable to perform in the previous case to work perfectly in the inner object types. Let's see how we can make the query with `"books.publisher": "penguin"` and `"books.genre": "scifi"`:

```
curl --XPOST localhost:9200/authors/nested_author/_search -d '
{
  "query": {
    "filtered": {
      "query": {"match_all": {}},
      "filter": {
        "nested": {
          "path": "books",
          "query":{
            "filtered": {
              "query": { "match_all": {}},
              "filter": {
                "and": [
                    {"term": {"books.publisher": "penguin"}},
                    {"term": {"books.genre": "scifi"}}
                ]
              }
            }
          }
        }
      }
    }
  }
}'
```

This would return the perfectly matched results that we are looking for.

Can the nested type solve all of your problems then? What is the downside of using a nested datatype? We will see that in the next section.

Limitations on a query on nested fields

There are some limitations to the nested object type. In the simple inner object type, each nested JSON object is treated independently. However, the act of defining the mapping for inner objects as a nested type lets you overcome this drawback. Also, the use of nested types has its disadvantages, which we are about to see:

- Nested types are updation unfriendly. Updating the parent element information or child element information means that you need to reindex the whole document. Hence, if a new student is admitted to a school or when a new student leaves the school, the entire document has to be reindexed, along with the information of other students and the school. Remember, updating a document is nothing but a soft deletion and addition of documents under the hood.

- You can't retrieve the nested object alone. Say you need to get information of a single student; this is not possible in this approach. You need to get the entire source of the document, which includes the information of the school and students, to check the data of a specific student.

Using a parent-child approach

A parent-child datatype is yet another alternative to establish relational data. In the parent-child approach, we establish the parent-child relation during index time. In a map reduce or sharded architecture, it's not possible for a map or shard to communicate with each other. The work has to be done independently by each shard. Keeping that in mind, relational data can't be maintained as a cross shard, which means I can't have the school information document in one shard and student information in another.

Hence, to establish a parent-child relation, it's required that the parent and child documents be in the same shard. Let's first see how to index parent and child documents and then how this rule is imposed.

Let's index some documents first. The index and type names are posts and post, respectively and the IDs corresponding them are manually given as 1, 2, and 3, as shown in the following code:

```
curl -XPOST localhost:9200/posts/post/1 -d '{
   "question":" elasticsearch query to return all records"
}'
curl -XPOST localhost:9200/posts/post/2 -d '{
  "question":" Elasticsearch, Sphinx, Lucene, Solr, Xapian. Which
  fits for which usage?"
}'
```

```
curl -XPOST localhost:9200/posts/post/3 -d '{
  "question":" Queries vs. Filters"
}
```

The preceding snippet indexed the author part as the parent document. Now, let's configure the mapping for the child document type:

```
curl -XPOST localhost:9200/posts/rating/_mapping -d '{
  "rating":{
    "_parent": {"type": "post"}
  }
}'
```

We created two types, namely `"post"` and `"rating"`, in the index named `"post"`. What the preceding code snippet does is that it maps the type `"post"` as the parent of the other type `"rating"`.

Now, whenever we index a child document, we mention an identifier to denote it as the child of a specific parent, as shown in the following code:

```
curl -XPOST localhost:9200/posts/rating/1?parent=1 -d '{
  "accepted":"yes",
  "rating":72,
  "answer":"http://localhost:9200/foo/_search?pretty=true&q=*:*"
}'
curl -XPOST localhost:9200/posts/rating/2?parent=1 -d '{
  "accepted":"yes",
  "rating":3,
  "answer":"curl -XGET localhost:9200/foo/_search?"
}'
curl -XPOST localhost:9200/posts/rating/3?parent=1 -d '{
  "accepted":"yes",
  "rating":2,
  "answer":http://127.0.0.1:9200/foo/_search/?size=1000&pretty=1\
}'
curl -XPOST localhost:9200/posts/rating/4?parent=1 -d '{
  "accepted":"yes",
  "rating":1,
  "answer":"elasticsearch.org/guide/reference/api/search/uri-
  request"
}'
curl -XPOST localhost:9200/posts/rating/5?parent=2 -d '{
  "accepted":"yes",
  "rating":10,
  "answer":"An experiment to compare Elasticsearch and Solr"
}'
```

```
curl -XPOST localhost:9200/posts/rating/6?parent=2 -d '{
  "accepted":"yes",
  "rating":8,
  "answer":"http://blog.socialcast.com/realtime-search-solr-vs-
  elasticsearch/"
}'
curl -XPOST localhost:9200/posts/rating/7?parent=2 -d '{
  "accepted":"yes",
  "rating":6,
  "answer":"Solr vs elasticsearch Deathmatch!"
}'
curl -XPOST localhost:9200/posts/rating/8?parent=3 -d '{
  "accepted":"yes",
  "rating":54,
  "answer":"filters are cached and dont influence the score,
  therefore faster than queries"
}'
curl -XPOST localhost:9200/posts/rating/9?parent=3 -d '{
  "accepted":"yes",
  "rating":2,
  "answer":"filters should be used instead of queries for
  binary yes/no searches and for queries on exact values"
}'
```

By indexing the child document with the parent ID, the parent-child relation is established. Now, under the hood, Elasticsearch needs to ensure that the parent and children documents are indexed in the same shard. For this, Elasticsearch uses routing. When a document is given for indexing, Elasticsearch needs to find to which shard that document should be mapped. Based on the document ID of the document, Elasticsearch uses a modulus function to find the shard. This is called routing and by default, the routing key is a document ID. In a parent-child scenario, the routing key for the child document is taken from the parent ID and Elasticsearch ensures that the parent and child documents go to the same shard.

The has_parent filter/the has_parent query

This query/filter works on the parent documents and returns the child documents.

The has_child query/the has_child filter

The has_child filter accepts a query and the child type to run against the query and this results in parent documents that have child docs matching the query. The has_child query also works like a has_child filter.

The top_children query

This query returns the top *n* number of children.

There is no strong connection between the parent and child documents in Elasticsearch. This lets you update a child or parent without affecting the whole document. Thus, the large memory overhead in the case of updation of documents can be avoided. However, this comes with a minimal performance cost since they are not directed to the same shard. To make use of the cache, the child documents are all routed to the same shard.

Schema design to store questions and answers

Using parent-child documents, we can easily find answers to questions and similarly, to questions that have a specific answer. Let's see how we can design such a schema in this section.

Imagine we have a forum like stackoverflow, where users can ask questions. Let's assume we are setting up such a schema in an index called "post".

First, let's create the index "post":

```
curl -XPOST localhost:9200/posts
```

We created a posts index to which we index the posts by users. Now, let's give our Elasticsearch instance an insight of what we will do by defining the mapping:

```
curl -XPOST localhost:9200/posts/rating/_mapping -d '{
  "rating":{
    "_parent": {"type": "post"}
  }
}'
```

As explained earlier, here we are mapping the type "post" as the parent of the type "rating".

Now, let's index our parent and child documents:

```
// Already indexed
```

With this, we have set up the schema design to store questions and answers.

Now, let's look into a requirement. It's required for a company to create a question and answer forum like stackoverflow, where questions can be posted and its answers can be given. Any person can come back and answer these questions. The same question can be answered by one or more person. So, the people who posted the question can see them and mark the most appropriate answer as the **accepted** answer. Also, the answers can be given an upvote or downvote by the users. The following points sum up the requirements of the site:

- Find all questions whose answer is accepted
- Find top questions whose upvotes for the answers are maximum
- Find the accepted answers of questions in order of question upvotes
- Find questions that have minimum three answers

Searching questions based on a criteria of answers

With the indexed set of documents, let's say, we need to find out how many answers for a particular question got a rating of greater than 50. Let's try to find that out by issuing a query:

```
curl -XPOST localhost:9200/posts/post/_search -d '{
  "query": {
    "filtered": {
      "query": {
        "text": {"question": " elasticsearch query to return all
        records "}
      },
      "filter":{
        "has_child": {
          "type": "rating",
          "query" : {
            "filtered": {
              "query": { "match_all": {}},
              "filter" : {
                "and": [
                  {"term": {"accepted": yes}},
                  {"range": {"rating": {"gt" : 50}}}
                ]
              }
            }
          }
        }
```

```
          }
        }
      }
    }
  }'
```

Searching answers based on a criteria of questions

Let's now try to find the parents by querying against the child docs, which is the reverse of what we did in the previous section. Take a look at this query:

```
curl -XPOST localhost:9200/posts/rating/_search?pretty=true -d '{
  "query": {
    "filtered": {
      "query": {"match_all": {}},
      "filter": {
        "and": [
          {"term": {"accepted": yes}},
          {
            "has_parent": {
              "type": "post",
              "query": {
                "term": {"question": " Queries vs. Filters "}
              }
            }
          }
        ]
      }
    }
  },
  "sort": [
    { "rating" : {"order" : "desc"} }
  ]
}'
```

Here, we get all the ratings whose question contains the term Queries vs. Filters in a descending order.

The score of questions based on the score of each answer

As there are different answers for each question and each query matches against each answer, there should be some mechanism to aggregate the score of each answer to form a final score for the parent, that is, the question:

```
curl -XPOST 'localhost:9200/posts/post/_search' -d '{
  "query": {
    "has_child": {
      "type": "rating",
      "query": {
        "function_score": {
          "functions": [
            {
              "field_value_factor": {
                "field": "rating"
              }
            }
          ]
        }
      },
      "score_mode": "sum"
    }
  }
}'
```

And the output is as follows:

```
{
  "took" : 5,
  "timed_out" : false,
  "_shards" : {
    "total" : 5,
    "successful" : 5,
    "failed" : 0
  },
  "hits" : {
    "total" : 3,
    "max_score" : 78.0,
    "hits" : [ {
      "_index" : "posts",
      "_type" : "post",
      "_id" : "1",
```

```
      "_score" : 78.0,
      "_source":{ "question": " elasticsearch query to return all
      records " }
   }, {
      "_index" : "posts",
      "_type" : "post",
      "_id" : "3",
      "_score" : 56.0,
      "_source":{ "question": " Queries vs. Filters " }
   }, {
      "_index" : "posts",
      "_type" : "post",
      "_id" : "2",
      "_score" : 24.0,
      "_source":{ "question" : " Elasticsearch, Sphinx, Lucene,
      Solr, Xapian. Which fits for which usage? " }
   } ]
   }
}
```

Here in the response, we can see that there is a field called _score, which we calculated using the preceding query, that we took as the sort criterion.

Filtering questions with more than four answers

Next, let's see how we can filter questions that have at least four answers. For this, there is a provision to filter parent documents based on the number of children they have. We can use the min_children attribute to implement this limit:

```
curl -XPOST 'localhost:9200/posts/post/_search' -d '{
  "query": {
    "has_child": {
      "type": "rating",
      "min_children": 4,
      "query": {
        "match_all": {}
      }
    }
  }
}'
```

Here, we are telling Elasticsearch to give all parent documents at least four children.

With this, we get the following result:

```
{
  "took" : 3,
  "timed_out" : false,
  "_shards" : {
    "total" : 5,
    "successful" : 5,
    "failed" : 0
  },
  "hits" : {
    "total" : 1,
    "max_score" : 1.0,
    "hits" : [ {
      "_index" : "posts",
      "_type" : "post",
      "_id" : "1",
      "_score" : 1.0,
      "_source":{ "question": " elasticsearch query to return all
      records " }
    } ]
  }
}
```

In the result, we can observe that only the questions that have at least four answers have appeared.

Similarly, we can use `max_children` attribute to mark the upper limit of children.

Displaying the best questions and their accepted answers

Now, let's get the top questions based on the number of votes it has and its accepted answers.

We can use inner object functionality in a parent-child relation to achieve this. This inner object functionality can be adding the `inner_hits` parameter to the query, as follows:

```
curl -XPOST 'localhost:9200/posts/post/_search' -d '{
  "query": {
    "has_child": {
      "type": "rating",
      "query": {
        "function_score": {
          "functions": [
```

```
              {
                "field_value_factor": {
                  "field": "rating"
                }
              }
            ]
          }
        },
        "score_mode": "sum",
        "inner_hits": {}
      }
    }
  }
}'
```

The output of the preceding query is shown here:

```
{
  "took": 11,
  "timed_out": false,
  "_shards": {
    "total": 5,
    "successful": 5,
    "failed": 0
  },
  "hits": {
    "total": 3,
    "max_score": 78,
    "hits": [
      {
        "_index": "posts",
        "_type": "post",
        "_id": "1",
        "_score": 78,
        "_source": {
          "question": " elasticsearch query to return all records
          "
        },
        "inner_hits": {
          "rating": {
            "hits": {
              "total": 4,
              "max_score": 72,
              "hits": [
                {
                  "_index": "posts",
                  "_type": "rating",
                  "_id": "1",
```

```
        "_score": 72,
        "_source": {
          "accepted": "yes",
          "rating": 72,
          "answer": "http://localhost:9200/foo/
          _search?pretty=true&q=*:*"
        }
      },
      {
        "_index": "posts",
        "_type": "rating",
        "_id": "2",
        "_score": 3,
        "_source": {
          "accepted": "yes",
          "rating": 3,
          "answer": "curl -XGET
          localhost:9200/foo/_search?"
        }
      },
      {
        "_index": "posts",
        "_type": "rating",
        "_id": "3",
        "_score": 2,
        "_source": {
        "accepted": "yes",
        "rating": 2,
        "answer": "http://127.0.0.1:9200/foo/_search/?
        size=1000&pretty=1"
        }
      }
    }
  ]
  }
 }
 }
},
{
  "_index": "posts",
  "_type": "post",
  "_id": "3",
  "_score": 56,
  "_source": {
    "question": " Queries vs. Filters "
  },
  "inner_hits": {
    "rating": {
```

```
"hits": {
  "total": 2,
  "max_score": 54,
  "hits": [
    {
      "_index": "posts",
      "_type": "rating",
      "_id": "8",
      "_score": 54,
      "_source": {
        "accepted": "yes",
        "rating": 54,
        "answer": "filters are cached and dont influence
        the score, therefore faster than queries"
      }
    },
    {
      "_index": "posts",
      "_type": "rating",
      "_id": "9",
      "_score": 2,
      "_source": {
        "accepted": "yes",
        "rating": 2,
        "answer": "filters should be used instead of
        queries for binary yes/no searches and for
        queries on exact values"
      }
    }
  ]
}
}
}
}
{
  "_index": "posts",
  "_type": "post",
  "_id": "2",
  "_score": 24,
  "_source": {
    "question": " ElasticSearch, Sphinx, Lucene, Solr, Xapian.
    Which fits for which usage? "
  },
  "inner_hits": {
    "rating": {
      "hits": {
        "total": 3,
```

```json
        "max_score": 10,
        "hits": [
          {
            "_index": "posts",
            "_type": "rating",
            "_id": "5",
            "_score": 10,
            "_source": {
              "accepted": "yes",
              "rating": 10,
              "answer": "An experiment to compare
              ElasticSearch and Solr"
            }
          },
          {
            "_index": "posts",
            "_type": "rating",
            "_id": "6",
            "_score": 8,
            "_source": {
              "accepted": "yes",
              "rating": 8,
              "answer": "http://blog.socialcast.com/realtime-
              search-solr-vs-elasticsearch/"
            }
          },
          {
            "_index": "posts",
            "_type": "rating",
            "_id": "7",
            "_score": 6,
            "_source": {
              "accepted": "yes",
              "rating": 6,
              "answer": "Solr vs elasticsearch Deathmatch!"
            }
          }
        ]
      }
    }
  }
  ]
}
}
```

Here, we can see that the results are sorted out on the basis of a score and for each result, inner hits are shown with the children that too are sorted on the basis of a score.

Note that the `inner_hits` parameter is supported only in Elasticsearch 1.5 and its higher versions.

Summary

In NoSQL, it's hard to establish relational data as data is scattered over various excluded buckets and you cannot interconnect them to process data.

However, Elasticsearch gives us various options to achieve this.

We saw that nested and parent-child structures give some good mechanisms to establish relational data. A cross comparison of these two approaches is as follows:

- A nested approach:
    - The data is joined by a design
    - This is ideal for cases with a smaller number of children
    - This is faster than the parent-child approach
    - Adding or deleting child means the entire document has to be reindexed, which is very costly in Lucene
    - Editing information of parent will also require a reindex, which is again very expensive

- A parent-child approach:
    - This works well for large number of children
    - This is ideal for large relations with a large number of children
    - Adding and deleting a child is seamless and cheap
    - Editing parent information can be done without any updation on the child document
    - Parent child is a bit expensive as for each parent query, all child documents have to be loaded in the main memory
    - We also saw the inner-hits parameter added in Elasticsearch versions 1.5 and its higher versions, which enables us not only to get the parents but also their respective children documents

In the next chapter, we will see the capability and usage of Elasticsearch in the analytics area with a few use case scenarios.

5
Analytics Using Elasticsearch

Over the years, the digital world has witnessed a tremendous explosion of data. With storage space cost rapidly decreasing, the world becoming a smaller place, and the rise in communication technology, the amount of data that can be stored and processed has rocketed. As it is almost impossible for human beings to make sense of this much data manually, the requirement for data analytics was born.

With petabytes of data sitting in their databases, users come up with use cases where they could crunch their data and bring in some great observations and powerful insight. This information could later be converted to insights on the basis of which we could take actions for the business and management world. This particular technology has wide spread application over a variety of domains. Retailers can use such insight to understand the preferences, trends, and usage patterns of customers to improve their services. In finance, data analytics could be used to monitor the finance news, blogs, and general sentiment of people towards a company to predict its stock activities. In the field of mobile telephony, analytics can be used to understand the postpaid recharging behavior of a user by tracking his usage level, and such information could be used to push users to the next usage level by offering them apt discounts at the right time. In politics, data analytics technology can be used to monitor social media and news to understand the general sentiments of people towards a political party.

Hence, we have a variety of use cases for analytics. What makes Elasticsearch special with respect to analytics is its ability to handle huge datasets and its ability to apply analytics over it at the same time. In this chapter, we will take airplane ticket booking as our use case / application and see how Elasticsearch fits into it to help the management better understand their customers to build a better business prospect out of this.

A flight ticket analytics scenario

A flight booking agency can find data analytics very important to improve its business. It has the following information per booked ticket about the passenger and the flight:

- The time of booking
- The time of flight departure
- The time of flight arrival
- The airport from which the plane departs
- The airport at which the plane arrives
- Whether the passenger is male or female
- The purpose of his/her visit
- Whether the passenger is travelling economy or business class

So, with this information, we can model the document in JSON, as follows:

```
{
    "departure" : {
      "time" : "2014-10-10 01:01:01",
      "airport" : "Kochi",
    },
    "arrival" : {
      "time" : "2014-10-10 01:01:01",
      "airport" : "Bangalore",
    }.
    "passengerDetails" : {
      "name" : "Damodar Das",
      "purposeOfVisit" : "WorkRelated",
      "sex" : "Male"
    },
    "ticketType" : "Business",
    "timeOfBooking" : "2014-09-09 09:09:01"
}
```

Index creation and mapping

Elasticsearch is schemaless, which means that you don't have to declare the schema and index the document. Instead, while indexing the document, it identifies the type for each field and creates the mapping. Here, the type of a field refers to how Elasticsearch should treat a data item, as a string, number, date, or something else. Although Elasticsearch guesses the type of each field while indexing data, its autodetected mapping might not be enough for us in many scenarios. To leverage date-related operations, such as a date range query and date aggregations, it's only intuitive to define these fields in a field type, which Elasticsearch understands as a date field type and is aware of its date value.

So, based on our requirements, we can define our schema as follows:

```bash
#!/bin/bash

if [ -z $1 ] ; then
    echo "Please enter hostname"
    exit
fi

hostname=$1

curl -X PUT "http://$hostname:9200/planeticketing" -d '{
        "index": {
            "number_of_shards": 2,
            "number_of_replicas": 1
        }
    }'

curl -X PUT "http://$hostname:9200/planeticketing/ticket
  /_mapping" -d '{
    "ticket" : {
    "properties" : {
        "ticketType" : { "type" : "string" , "index" :
          "not_analyzed" },
        "timeOfBooking" : { "type" : "date", "format" :
          "YYYY-MM-dd HH:mm:ss"},
        "departure" : {
            "properties" : {
                "airport" : { "type" : "string" },
                "time" : { "type" : "date", "format" :
                  "YYYY-MM-dd HH:mm:ss"}
            }
        },
```

```
        "arrival" : {
            "properties" : {
                "airport" : { "type" : "string" },
                "time" : { "type" : "date", "format" :
                  "YYYY-MM-dd HH:mm:ss"}
            }
        },
        "passengerDetails" : {
            "properties" : {
                "name" : { "type" : "string" },
                "purposeOfVisit" : { "type" : "string",
                  "index" : "not_analyzed"  },
                "sex" : { "type" : "string", "index" :
                  "not_analyzed" }
            }
        }
    }}
}'
```

First, we created an index called `planeticketing` and assigned two shards and one replica to it. The replica makes sure that even if one machine goes down in the network at a time, the cluster will cope up with the situation and make sure that the search cluster remains available for search without any downtime.

Next, we defined the schema. Note that for most of the fields that have a string value, such as `sex`, `purposeOfVisit`, and so on, we add the `not_analyzed` field type definition. Defining the index attribute as `not_analzed` makes sure that the search for the exact match works for the field. This makes sure that these fields are not tokenized or lowercased for indexing and makes sure that while aggregation, we can aggregate the raw/actual value rather than broken-down tokens, which would give us weird results.

Index configuration as `not_analyzed` will make sure that the string is not tokenized before it reaches the reverse index. Using this, we can get the exact match and also, get aggregation on the actual string rather than the tokenized string. You should also note that we can also configure a field so that it is not searchable when we set the index value as `no`. In this case, none of the tokens in the string go to the reverse index.

We have adopted the time format `YYYY-MM-dd HH:mm:ss` for all the date time fields. This information needs to be provided to Elasticsearch so that it understands the date strings given in JSON (how it interprets and stores it in the date format).

A case study on analytics requirements

The agency feels that it needs to monitor the distribution of tickets booked over time. It comes up with a set of analytic reports that it is interested in. Visualization always helps to grasp an idea in a single view and the firm believes that visualization of these values would give them better value than just the raw value.

Thus, the firm comes up with the following analysis for weekly reports, which we will discuss in more detail further in this chapter:

- Male and female distribution of passengers.
- Trend of booking tickets.
- Correlation of departure and arrival of flights at airports.
- Correlation of ticket type with time.
- Most preferred hour for booking tickets.
- Most preferred weekday for travel.
- Correlation between passenger's purpose of visit, ticket type, and their sex.

Male and female distribution of passengers

First, let's start with a simple problem. The management wants to see the ratio of male and female passengers. We can run the terms aggregation on the `passengerDetails.sex` field. This will return the number of male passengers and female passengers.

The Elasticsearch query is as follows:

```
{
  "query": {
    "range": {
      "timeOfBooking": {
        "gte": "2014-09-01 00:00:00",
        // => We are applying analytics on one month worth data
        "lt": "2014-10-01 00:00:00"
      }
    }
  },
  "aggregations": {
    "maleToFemale": {
```

```
        "terms": {
          "field": "passengerDetails.sex"
          // => Apply aggregation on sex field
        }
      }
    }
  }
```

The following is the response of the preceding query:

```
    "aggregations" : {
      "maleToFemale" : {
        "buckets" : [
              {  "key" : "Male",   "doc_count" : 3  },
              { "key" : "Female",    "doc_count" : 1  }
          ]
        }
      }
    }
```

Finally, let's visualize the response using a pie chart:

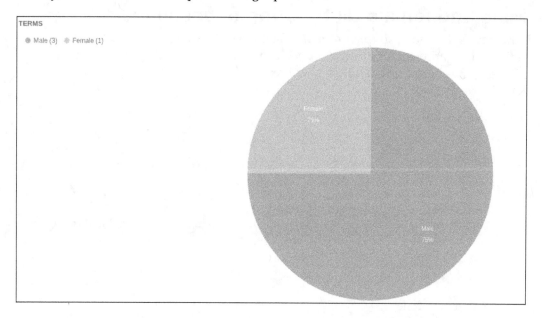

 You should note that, here, the scope of aggregation is in the query. This means that aggregation happens only on documents that match the query.

The inference: It was observed that more male passengers preferred to travel by airplane over female passengers. This ratio came in at 1:4 where the lower ratio refers to the female passengers and the higher ratio refers to the male passengers.

Time-based patterns or trends in booking tickets

The problem: The management wants to study what are the probable timings when the majority of travelers book tickets. Depending on these stats, they will add new servers or additional support at peak hours to ease the process of booking. Also, they want to correlate the holidays with the time of booking to check whether they can roll out any additional offers for the travelers.

How to solve it: Elasticsearch provides the date histogram aggregation using which we can aggregate dates over a given granularity. This granularity can be of an hour, minute, month, or even seconds. Elasticsearch also supports other formats, such as 1.5 days, 3.5 months, and so on.

The Elasticsearch query is as follows:

```
{
  "query": {
    "range": {
      "timeOfBooking": {
        "gte": "2014-09-01 00:00:00",
        "lt": "2014-10-01 00:00:00"
      }
    }
  },
  "aggregations": {
    "ticketTrends": {
      "date_histogram": {
        "field": "timeOfBooking",
        "interval": "day"
      }
    }
  }
}
```

The following is the response of the preceding query:

```
"aggregations" : {
  "ticketTrends" : {
    "buckets" : [ {
        "key_as_string" : "2014-09-09 00:00:00",
        "key" : 1410220800000,
```

```
            "doc_count" : 3
     }, {
            "key_as_string" : "2014-09-21 00:00:00",
            "key" : 1411257600000,
            "doc_count" : 1
     } ]
   }
}
```

The analytic inference: We received various hours and the document count corresponding to each hour. For each hour, we received the epoch for the start of the hour as a key field and the date string representation as the `key_as_string` field.

A normal bar graph with *x* axis as time would be the best way to represent this information, as shown in the following graph:

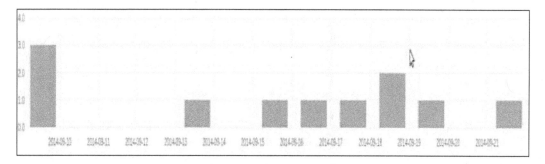

Hottest arrival and departure points

The problem: The management wants to study flight departure and arrival trends at airports to understand where the maximum number of departures and arrivals occurs. Depending on the data, they want to roll out offers like discounts and want to add more flights to that route.

How to solve it: The beauty of aggregations in Elasticsearch is that you can nest the aggregations inside another aggregation. This means that you can do a term aggregation nested in another term aggregation or any other aggregation type. This can increase the number of levels of the aggregation nesting and can make it deep. Here, we have a two-level aggregation with the first level as a term aggregation over the city from where the flight departs. At the second level, we mark the arrival city as a term aggregation. This combination gives us the list of top departure cities and top arrival cities for each departure city.

This is the Elasticsearch query:

```json
{
    "query": {
      "range": {
        "timeOfBooking": {
          "gte": "2014-09-01 00:00:00",
          "lt": "2014-10-01 00:00:00"
        }
      }
    },
    "aggregations": {
      "departure": {
        "terms": {
          "field": "departure.airport"
        },
        "aggregations": {
            "arrival": {
                "terms": {
                    "field": "arrival.airport"
                }
            }
          }
        }
      }
    }
}
```

The following is the response of the preceding query:

```json
"aggregations" : {
    "departure" : {
      "buckets" : [ {
        "key" : "kochi",
        "doc_count" : 3,
          "arrival" : {
              "buckets" : [ {
                  "key" : "delhi",
                  "doc_count" : 2
                }, {
                  "key" : "bangalore",
                  "doc_count" : 1
                } ]
            }
      }, {
        "key" : "banglore",
```

```
              "doc_count" : 1,
                  "arrival" : {
                     "buckets" : [ {
                          "key" : "delhi",
                          "doc_count" : 1
                     } ]
                  }
            } ]
         }
      }
   }
```

The following is the visual representation of the preceding response:

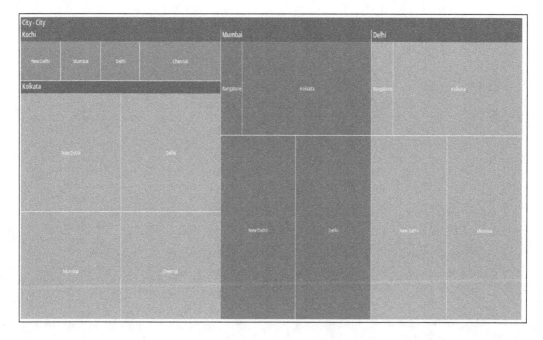

The analytic inference: We received the top cities from where tickets were booked and the top cities to which each of these cities are connected. We represented this information neatly using a tree map.

The correlation of ticket type with time

Problem: Currently, there are two kinds of tickets based on the services offered by the agency in the plan: business class and economy class. In business class, more attention is given to the passenger and he/she is offered good food and even drinks. However, the management noted that the fixed number of seats for business and economy class didn't pay off well. At times, economy seats got filled, but business class seats remained unoccupied. Again, if they had allocated those seats to economy instead of business class, they would have got better revenue out of a flight. With the possibility of dynamically allocating seats between business and economy class, the management is interested understanding the monthly seat occupancy trends.

Depending on this trend, they can preset the number of seats for each class and get better revenue.

How to solve it: We can use the nested aggregation capability of Elasticsearch to solve this issue. A two-level aggregation with the date histogram aggregation on the timeOfBooking field will constitute the base level of aggregation. Term aggregation of the ticketType field on top of the date aggregation will give us our required results.

This is the Elasticsearch query:

```
{
  "query": {
    "range": {
      "timeOfBooking": {
        "gte": "2014-09-01 00:00:00",
        "lt": "2014-10-01 00:00:00"
      }
    }
  },
  "aggregations": {
    "ticketTrends": {
      "date_histogram": {
        "field": "timeOfBooking",
        "interval": "day"
      },
      "aggs": {
        "ticketType": {
          "terms": {
            "field": "ticketType"
          }
        }
      }
    }
  }
}
```

The following is the response of the preceding query:

```
"aggregations" : {
  "ticketTrends" : {
    "buckets" : [ {
      "key_as_string" : "2014-09-09 00:00:00",
      "key" : 1410220800000,
      "doc_count" : 3,
      "ticketType" : {
        "buckets" : [ {
          "key" : "Ecnomical",
          "doc_count" : 2
        }, {
          "key" : "Business",
          "doc_count" : 1
        } ]
      }
    }, {
      "key_as_string" : "2014-09-13 00:00:00",
      "key" : 1410566400000,
      "doc_count" : 1,
      "ticketType" : {
        "buckets" : [ {
          "key" : "Business",
          "doc_count" : 1
        } ]
      }
    } , { …. } , {…..} ,
    }
  }
}
```

This graph provides you with a visual representation of the preceding response:

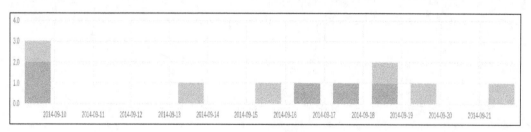

The analytic inference: It can be concluded that at the start of the month and in the middle of the month, a lot of business class tickets are booked, but then later on, this goes down and economy class tickets are preferred.

Distribution of the travel duration

Problem: An external flight booking company came to the management claiming that if it lowers the price of short duration travel, it can reap a small profit out of it, but more importantly, it would make the journey more comfortable for passengers, thereby making them want to travel by plane more. Their theory was that if someone starts travelling by plane, they will feel uncomfortable to travel by a normal train or bus. So, even though a reduced tariff for a short journey might not prove to be very profitable, it might help attract more passengers so that they use planes for their daily travel. Seeing a definite edge to this proposal, the management asked the analytics team to give statistics on the time duration of travel. The management needs to see whether shorter duration travel is preferred and if not, by what margin.

How to solve it: The flexibility in aggregation lies in its hooks for scripts. Elasticsearch offers scripting support on various languages, such as Groovy, JavaScript, and Python.

 MVEL was depreciated and removed from Elasticsearch 1.4.0. Due to its sandboxing capabilities and faster execution, Groovy is the default and preferred language of Elasticsearch.

Elasticsearch exposes various data hooks for such custom scripts, where field values from indexed documents can be referenced and other properties, such as a term's inverse document frequency, are also made available. Here, we will use this script hook to access the arrival and departure date fields. These values when subtracted will give the duration of travel. But remember that like most other applications and languages, Elasticsearch stores a date as epoch. Which means that on accessing the date value, you will actually get the epoch representation of that time. Thus, on subtracting these date/time fields, we should get the duration of a flight in epoch.

 This is the mathematical formula (in code) to calculate it:
```
def timeDiff = doc['arrival.time'].value -
doc['departure.time'].value ;
return  Math.round( timeDiff/(1000 * 100 * 60 ))
```

We later find the corresponding hours of this epoch representation. This value is then aggregated to find the frequency of each duration.

The Elasticsearch request is as follows:

```
{
  "query": {
    "range": {
      "timeOfBooking": {
        "gte": "2014-09-01 00:00:00",
        "lt": "2014-10-01 00:00:00"
      }
    }
  },
  "aggregations": {
    "ticketTrends": {
      "terms": {
        "script": "def timeDiff = doc['arrival.time'].
          value -  doc['departure.time'].value ;
          Math.round( timeDiff/(1000 * 100 * 60 ))   ",
        "lang": "groovy"
      }
    }
  }
}
```

The following is the response of the preceding query:

```
"aggregations" : {
  "ticketTrends" : {
    "buckets" : [ {
          "key" : "2",
          "doc_count" : 1
      }, {
          "key" : "1",
          "doc_count" : 2
      }, {
          "key" : "3",
          "doc_count" : 4
    }, {
          "key" : "10,
          "doc_count" : 10
      }, {
          "key" : "21",
          "doc_count" : 12
      } ]
    }
  }
```

The following graph provides you with a visual representation of the preceding response:

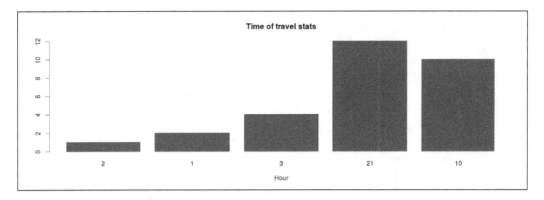

Analytic inference: We noted that planes are not much used for short duration travel. People prefer cheaper modes of transport for short duration travel.

The most preferred or hottest hour for booking tickets

Problem: The server maintenance team notified the management that at times, the load on the server is too high and at times, the load is marginal. To serve the traffic better at the time when there is a peak load, it needs more machines. The management feels that if it can track the peak hours when the majority of tickets are booked, it can pay more attention to the trend of booking around that time. The management also wants to verify the claims of the server maintenance team and if they're proved correct, add more machines to handle the load.

Hence, the management has come back to us asking for data on hourly distribution of the site traffic.

How to solve it: We use the script hooks provided to us to convert a date to its particular hour. Aggregating this value gives us the distribution of hour of the day to the number of bookings for that day.

The code used to get the date is as follows:
```
def mydate = new Date(doc['timeOfBooking'].value);
return mydate.format('HH')",
```

The following is the Elasticsearch request:

```
{
  "query": {
    "range": {
      "timeOfBooking": {
        "gte": "2014-09-01 00:00:00",
        "lt": "2014-10-01 00:00:00"
      }
    }
  },
  "aggregations": {
    "ticketTrends": {
      "terms": {
        "script": "def mydate = new Date
          (doc['timeOfBooking'].value); mydate.format('HH')",
        "lang": "groovy"
      }
    }
  }
}
```

This is the response of the preceding query:

```
"aggregations" : {
  "ticketTrends" : {
    "buckets" : [ {
      "key" : "14",
      "doc_count" : 9
    }, {
      "key" : "02",
      "doc_count" : 1
    }, {
      "key" : "08",
      "doc_count" : 1
    } ,
{ .... } , { .... }
]
    }
  }
}
```

The following graph shows the visual representation of the preceding response:

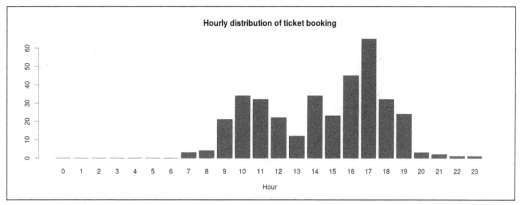

Analytic inference: We note that booking is more active during the evening hours and towards the end of business hours.

The most preferred or hottest weekday for travel

Problem: The management noted that there was a trend in ticket booking based on weekdays. They feel that they need to capture this trend so that they find some insight regarding it on the basis of which we can take the required actions in future.

How to solve it: Though we have the date, we haven't stored it in a day of a week format. For this purpose, we can use script support of Elasticsearch to get the corresponding day of week for each date.

 This is the code that is used to get the day of the week:

```
def mydate = new Date(doc[''timeOfBooking'].value);
return  mydate.format('EEEEEE')";
```

Here, we will extract the date value and convert it to a groovy date object. We use the standard date format to convert this object to the day of week string value.

The following is the Elasticsearch request:

```
{
   "query": {
     "range": {
       "timeOfBooking": {
         "gte": "2014-09-01 00:00:00",
         "lt": "2014-10-01 00:00:00"
       }
```

```
      }
    },
    "aggregations": {
      "ticketTrends": {
        "terms": {
          "script": "def mydate =
            new Date(doc[''timeOfBooking'].value);
            mydate.format('EEEEEE')",
          "lang": "groovy"
        }
      }
    }
  }
```

The following is the response of the preceding query:

```
    "aggregations" : {
      "ticketTrends" : {
        "buckets" : [ {
          "key" : "Tuesday",
          "doc_count" : 3
        }, {
          "key" : "Thursday",
          "doc_count" : 2
        }, {
          "key" : "Wednesday",
          "doc_count" : 2
        }, {
          "key" : "Friday",
          "doc_count" : 1
        }, {
          "key" : "Monday",
          "doc_count" : 1
        }, {
          "key" : "Saturday",
          "doc_count" : 1
        }, {
          "key" : "Sunday",
          "doc_count" : 1
        } ]
      }
    }
```

The following graph shows you the visual representation of the preceding response:

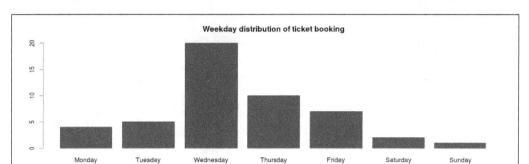

Analytic inference: We note here that most of the bookings were made on Wednesdays.

The pattern between a passenger's purpose of visit, ticket type, and their sex

Problem: In a rare case, the management felt that there might be a strong correlation between a passenger's purpose of visit, the ticket type, and passenger's sex. As a research case, they would like to check whether there exists any correlation between all three. It has noted a strong correlation between all these three dimensions and it feels that it needs to capture it in numbers.

How to solve it: As discussed previously, we can do any level of nested aggregations. This means that to achieve our current objective, all we need to do is craft a three-level aggregation with the purposeOfVisit field on the first level, ticketType on the second level, and the sex field on the third level.

The following is the Elasticsearch request:

```
{
  "query": {
    "range": {
      "timeOfBooking": {
        "gte": "2014-09-01 00:00:00",
        "lt": "2014-10-01 00:00:00"
      }
    }
  },
  "aggregations": {
    "purposeOfVisit": {
      "terms": {
        "field": "passengerDetails.purposeOfVisit"
```

```
        },
        "
    aggregations
    ": {
      "ticketType": {
          "terms": {
              "field": "ticketType"
          },
          "aggs": {
              "sex": {
                  "terms": {
                      "field": "sex"
                  }
              }
          }
        }
      }
    }
  }
}
```

This is the response of the preceding query:

```
    "aggregations" : {
      "purposeOfVisit" : {
        "buckets" : [ {
          "key" : "WorkRelated",
          "doc_count" : 6,
          "ticketType" : {
            "buckets" : [ {
              "key" : "Business",
              "doc_count" : 6,
              "sex" : {
                "buckets" : [ {
                  "key" : "Male",
                  "doc_count" : 6
                } ]
              }
            } ]
          }
        }, {
          "key" : "Personal",
          "doc_count" : 5,
          "ticketType" : {
            "buckets" : [ {
              "key" : "Business",
              "doc_count" : 3,
              "sex" : {
                "buckets" : [ {
                  "key" : "Male",
```

```
                    "doc_count" : 3
                } ]
            }
        }, {
            "key" : "Ecnomical",
            "doc_count" : 2,
            "sex" : {
                "buckets" : [ {
                    "key" : "Female",
                    "doc_count" : 1
                }, {
                    "key" : "Male",
                    "doc_count" : 1
                } ]
            }
        } ]
    }
} ]
    }
    }
}
```

The following pie chart gives you the visual representation of the preceding response:

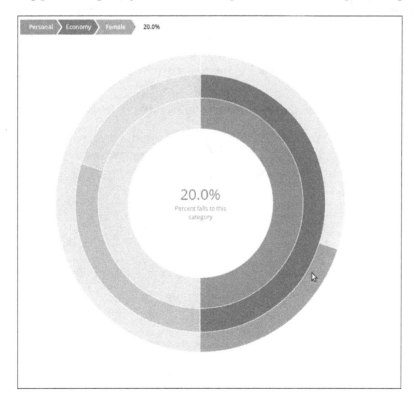

Analytic inference: In this particular case, we observed that business type tickets and preferences are closely related.

Summary

The core value of Elasticsearch is to run queries and analytics on top of it. All these in real time make Elasticsearch a unique and widely used combination. Here, real time refers to the ability of Elasticsearch to ingest documents one at a time and to make the document searchable immediately once it's given for indexing. Elasticsearch has a wide range of analytic features as its innate support. From day one, it was built in such a way that all these features could be rendered in real time. It has to also be noted that the scope of aggregation is its query score. This means that the input of the aggregation is the output of the query. The documents matching the query are passed through the aggregation to get the aggregation result.

The highlights of this chapter are as follows:

- Nested aggregations can be used to club various aggregations, such as terms, geo, date histogram, and so on, to solve analytics requirements in many cases. This core feature, once mastered properly, can be used to solve many domain-specific aggregations and analytic requirements.

- Elasticsearch provides various script hooks. It has support for Groovy, Python, and JavaScript. MVEL was the default language previously, but has been removed in version 1.4.0 due to security issues. Groovy is the default language now.

- Nested aggregation can be done to any number of levels.

In the coming chapter, you will learn how to improve the search quality of text search. This includes a description of various analyzers and a detailed description of how to mix and match them.

6
Improving the Search Experience

Once we have the search in place, we need to improve the entire search experience. Improving the search experience means to provide a hassle-free and seamless search and the ability to get results for the user on the first try. In various contexts, this might mean differently. In some situations, considering the synonyms of the search term might help the user better. In other situations, providing a provision to search an e-mail or link in an unstructured text might help the user more. In short, the search engine should be able to guess what the user is searching for even if the user hasn't provided the right term to search.

In this chapter, we will explore various search patterns from a user's perspective and then, we'll go further to understand how these patterns arise. Later on, we will focus on how to solve them with the help of internal and external analyzers and plugins developed for Elasticsearch.

News search

Let's consider a news vendor and their requirement to open up a news search portal. We are asked to create a user-friendly search for them.

For this, we will create some news per document and model the data around it:

- Document 1:

```
{
    "Title" : "Doctor opens online free consultation",
    "Content" : "Dr Malhotra offers his free
        consultation over the internet for patients.
        The patients can either logon to
        www.malhotra-help.com or mail him to
        malhotra@gmail.com" ,
```

```
            "Author" : "Anjali Shankar"
    }
```

- Document 2:

```
    {
            "Title" : "Online site for buying groceries",
            "Content" : :"Folks at Factweavers INC have
               opened at new site called
               www.buygroceriesonline.com for online
               purchase of local groceries.
               The purchase can also be done by mailing to
               buygroceries@gmail.com" ,
            "Author" : "Anjali shankar"
    }
```

- Document 3:

```
    {
            "Title" : "India launches Make In India  campaign",
            "Content" : :"PM of India inaugurates make
               in India campaign" ,
            "Author" : "Ram Shankar"
    }
```

A case-insensitive search

When we conduct a search, the search has to be case insensitive. This means that even if the user searches with capital letters in keywords, his/her search should avoid the casing of the characters and match keywords with any case. In short, the following should happen while indexing and searching:

```
    [ "ElasticSearch" , "elasticSearch" ] => "elasticsearch"
```

To enable a case-insensitive search, we need to design our analyzers accordingly. Once the analyzer is made, we need to simply apply it to the fields in the mapping. Let's see how we can achieve this:

1. First, we need to create the analyzer:

```
curl -X PUT "http://localhost:9200/news" -d '{
  "analysis": {
    "analyzer": {
      "lowercase": {
        "type": "custom",
        "tokenizer": "standard",
        "filter": [
          "lowercase"
        ]
```

```
        }
      }
    }
  }'
```

2. Then, we need to apply the analyzer to the required field:

```
curl -X PUT "http://localhost:9200/news/public/_mapping" -d '{
  "public": {
    "properties": {
      "Title": {
        "type": "string",
        "analyzer": "lowercase"
      },
      "Content": {
        "type": "string",
        "analyzer": "lowercase"
      }
    }
  }
}'
```

Once you have made the analyzer and assigned it the field in the mapping accordingly, any search to that particular field would be case insensitive. This is possible because by default, the analyzer applied on a field is used while indexing and searching.

> A term or terms query might not work even after applying an analyzer. This is because, for these queries, analyzers are not applied on the search side.

Effective e-mail or URL link search inside text

Let's search in the content field of the documents that we have for the e-mail address malhotra@gmail.com:

```
{
  "query" : {
    "match" : {
      "content" : "malhotra@gmail.com"
    }
  }
}
```

Incidentally, Document 1 and Document 2 matched our query rather than just Document 1.

Let's see why this happened and how:

- By default, the standard analyzer is taken as the default analyzer
- The standard analyzer breaks `malhotra@gmail.com` into malhotra and gmail.com
- The standard analyzer also breaks the e-mail ID `buygroceries@gmail.com` into buygroceries and gmail.com
- This means that when we search for the e-mail ID `malhotra@gmail.com`, either malhotra or gmail.com needs to match for the document to be qualified as a result

Hence, both Document 1 and Document 2 matched our query rather than just Document 1.

The solution for this problem is to use the **UAX Email URL** tokenizer rather than the default tokenizer. This tokenizer preserves e-mail IDs and URL links and won't break them. Hence our search works.

Let's see how we can make the analyzer for this:

```
curl -X PUT "http://localost:9200/news" -d '{
  "analysis": {
    "analyzer": {
      "urlAnalyzer": {
        "type": "custom",
        "tokenizer": "uax_url_email"
      }
    }
  }
}'
```

Finally, we need to apply it to our field:

```
curl -X PUT "http://$hostname:9200/news/public/_mapping" -d '{
  "public": {
    "properties": {
      "Content": {
        "type": "string",
        "analyzer": "urlAnalyzer"
      }
    }
  }
}'
```

Now, when tokenization happens, it won't break the tokens based on @. Hence, our previous condition won't prevail.

Prioritizing a title match over content match

It is often required that you conduct a search on multiple fields, but then, it's also important to make sure that certain field matches are prioritized over the others to make the search results more relevant.

If we are using a multifield search, it is a good idea to use a multisearch query. Here, you can give multiple fields and also prioritize on some of the fields. An example of this is as follows:

```
{
  "query": {
    "multi_match": {
      "query": "white elephant",
      "fields": [
        "Title^10",
        "Content"
      ]
    }
  }
}
```

Here, we search on both the `Title` and `Content` field and prioritize the `Title` field match over the `Content` field match. The `^10` parameter next to the `Title` field name makes sure that the match over the `Title` field is given 10 times more relevance.

Terms aggregation giving weird results

Let's consider an aggregation in the `Author` field to get the statistics of each author name:

```
curl -XPOST  "http://localhost:9200/news/public/
  _search?pretty&search_type=count" -d '{
    "aggs" : {
      "authors" : {
        "terms" : {
          "field" : "Author"
        }
      }
    }
  }'
```

By giving `search_type=count`, we make sure that we receive only the aggregation results and not hits or rather, the top-10 results.

The response we get for this is as follows:

```
{
  "took" : 5,
  "timed_out" : false,
  "_shards" : {
    "total" : 1,
    "successful" : 1,
    "failed" : 0
  },
  "hits" : {
    "total" : 3,
    "max_score" : 0.0,
    "hits" : [ ]
  },
  "aggregations" : {
    "authors" : {
      "doc_count_error_upper_bound" : 0,
      "sum_other_doc_count" : 0,
      "buckets" : [ {
        "key" : "shankar",
        "doc_count" : 3
      }, {
        "key" : "anjali",
        "doc_count" : 2
      }, {
        "key" : "ram",
        "doc_count" : 1
      } ]
    }
  }
}
```

Here, we see unexpected results. To understand what happens here, we need to understand how Elasticsearch works in depth. Elasticsearch is made on top of a powerful text search and analytics library called **Lucene**. Lucene creates a reverse index, where the words/tokens are reverse mapped to the documents they appeared in.

For instance, let's take the following two examples:

```
Doc-1 = "Elasticsearch is a great tool"
Doc-2 = "Elasticsearch is a search tool"
```

Now, let's create a reverse index based on these two documents:

```
Elasticsearch -> { Doc-1 , Doc-2}
great -> { Doc-1}
tool -> { Doc-1 , Doc-2}
```

Aggregation takes place in this broken token set rather than the plain text and hence, our result is broken into words instead of the exact text.

Now, let's see what we can do to counter this behavior.

Setting the field as not_analyzed

Our first option would be to bypass the analyzer for the author field. This can be achieved using the following setting in the mapping:

```
curl -X PUT "http://localhost:9200/news/public/_mapping" -d
'{
  "public": {
    "properties": {
      "Author": {
        "type": "string",
        "index": "not_analyzed"
      }
    }
  }
}'
```

After setting this new mapping and indexing all the documents, we can try our previous aggregation query. This query gives us the following response:

```
{
  "took" : 6,
  "timed_out" : false,
  "_shards" : {
    "total" : 1,
    "successful" : 1,
    "failed" : 0
  },
  "hits" : {
    "total" : 3,
    "max_score" : 0.0,
    "hits" : [ ]
  },
  "aggregations" : {
    "authors" : {
```

```
    "doc_count_error_upper_bound" : 0,
    "sum_other_doc_count" : 0,
    "buckets" : [ {
      "key" : "Anjali Shankar",
      "doc_count" : 1
    }, {
      "key" : "Anjali shankar",
      "doc_count" : 1
    }, {
      "key" : "Ram Shankar",
      "doc_count" : 1
    } ]
  }
 }
}
```

With these settings, the term aggregation went well, but then, if the case of the author name is different, we will get different results per case. This is not what we were asking for. We would also like to override the casing and would like to group the results as case insensitive.

In this case, it would be a good idea to create an analyzer of our own using the **keyword** tokenizer.

Using a lowercased analyzer

In the previous attempt, we noted that, though we were able to solve the problem partially, there were still issues with it. In this case, it would be a good approach to use the keyword tokenizer. The keyword tokenizer allows you to keep the text as it is before it reaches the filters.

> As opposed to the not_analyzed approach, the keyword tokenizer approach allows us to apply filters, such as lowercase, to the text.

Now, let's see how we can implement this analyzer.

First, we need to create our analyzer while creating the index:

```
curl -X PUT "http://localhost:9200/news" -d '{
  "analysis": {
    "analyzer": {
      "flat": {
        "type": "custom",
```

```
            "tokenizer": "keyword",
            "filter": "lowercase"
        }
    }
}
}'
```

Next in the mapping, we should map the flat analyzer we just made to the required field:

```
curl -X PUT "http://localhost:9200/news/public/_mapping" -d '{
  "public": {
    "properties": {
      "Author": {
        "type": "string",
        "analyzer": "flat"
      }
    }
  }
}'
```

Now, let's see the output to our query:

```
{
  "took" : 6,
  "timed_out" : false,
  "_shards" : {
    "total" : 1,
    "successful" : 1,
    "failed" : 0
  },
  "hits" : {
    "total" : 3,
    "max_score" : 0.0,
    "hits" : [ ]
  },
  "aggregations" : {
    "authors" : {
      "doc_count_error_upper_bound" : 0,
      "sum_other_doc_count" : 0,
      "buckets" : [ {
        "key" : "anjali shankar",
        "doc_count" : 2
      }, {
        "key" : "ram shankar",
```

```
        "doc_count" : 1
      } ]
    }
  }
}
```

The output looks good, but then the capital letters of the names are lost. However, the result looks good for us. We can titleize the result if required from the client side.

Improving the search experience using stemming

Stemming is the process where we convert an English word to its base form.

Some of the examples are shown as follows:

```
[ running , ran  ] => run
[ laughing ,  laugh , laughed ] => laugh
```

With this, our search would be a lot better. When someone searches for run, then all documents, no matter whether they consist the word running or ran, will also be shown as a match.

 This is possible because we apply the analyzer used for indexing on the search side too.

To achieve this, we have two approaches:

- **The algorithmic approach**: In this approach, we use a generic language-based algorithm to convert words to their stems or base form
- **The dictionary-based approach**: In this approach, we use a lookup mechanism to map the word to its base form

Let's see how the algorithmic approach can be implemented and what are its pros and cons.

Our first choice is the **snowball** algorithm. It's a powerful algorithm that finds the stem of a given word using an algorithm. This means that it intelligently removes trailing characters, such as ing, ed, and so on.

Let's see how to implement this algorithm and examine some of its output:

```
curl -X PUT "http://localhost:9200/news" -d '{
  "analysis": {
```

```
    "analyzer": {
      "stemmerAnalyzer": {
        "type": "custom",
        "tokenizer": "standard",
        "filter": [
          "lowercase",
          "snowball"
        ]
      }
    }
  }
}'
```

Now, let's examine how this analyzer breaks text into tokens. For this purpose, we can use the analyzer API. The analyzer API is meant for debugging purposes and can take an index analyzer as a parameter. This analyzer is applied on the payload text and the analyzed tokens are given back, as shown in the following code:

```
curl -XPOST 'localhost:9200/news/_analyze?analyzer
  =stemmerAnalyzer&pretty' -d 'running run'
{
  "tokens" : [ {
    "token" : "run",
    "start_offset" : 0,
    "end_offset" : 7,
    "type" : "<ALPHANUM>",
    "position" : 1
  }, {
    "token" : "run",
    "start_offset" : 8,
    "end_offset" : 11,
    "type" : "<ALPHANUM>",
    "position" : 2
  } ]
}
```

Here, we can see that the words "running" and "run" are mapped to their base forms, which is run. Now, let's see some complex examples. Let's see how snowball handles the `insider` and `inside` text:

```
curl -XPOST 'localhost:9200/news/_analyze?analyzer
  =stemmerAnalyzer&pretty' -d 'insider inside'
{
  "tokens" : [ {
    "token" : "insid",
    "start_offset" : 0,
```

```
      "end_offset" : 7,
      "type" : "<ALPHANUM>",
      "position" : 1
    }, {
      "token" : "insid",
      "start_offset" : 8,
      "end_offset" : 14,
      "type" : "<ALPHANUM>",
      "position" : 2
    } ]
  }
```

Now, the stemming of the word "running" went well, but the stem of `insider` looks rather funny. This is fine as long as we use the same word on the search query also. However, `insider` and `inside` are mapped to the same stem. Though `insider` looks similar to `inside`, it's an entirely different term with a different meaning. Hence, the algorithmic approach can fail in some cases.

> The snowball-algorithm-based stemming is fast, but not 100 percent accurate.

Hence, it would be a good idea to choose a dictionary-based approach. The **hunspell** filter can be used for this.

> The hunspell-dictionary-based stemming is 100 percent accurate, but will affect the search performance as the lookup has to take place on all searches.

A synonym-aware search

Elasticsearch considers synonyms while searching. This means that if you search for the word "big", a document would be matched even if any of the synonyms of the word big, such as "large", are present in that document.

Let's see how we can implement a simple synonym filter and how it works under the hood:

```
curl -X PUT "http://localhost:9200/news" -d '{
  "analysis": {
    "filter": {
      "synonym": {
        "type": "synonym",
        "synonyms": [
```

```
            "big, large",
            "round, circle"
          ]
        }
      },
      "analyzer": {
        "synonymAnalyzer": {
          "type": "custom",
          "tokenizer": "standard",
          "filter": [
            "lowercase",
            "synonym"
          ]
        }
      }
    }
  }
}'
```

Here, we created a synonym filter and provided a set of synonyms in it. Elasticsearch does not have a standard dictionary of synonyms so we need to provide it ourselves.

Let's apply our analyzer on some sample text using the analyzer API and examine the result:

```
curl -XPOST 'localhost:9200/news/_analyze?analyzer
  =synonymAnalyzer&pretty' -d 'big'
{
  "tokens" : [ {
    "token" : "big",
    "start_offset" : 0,
    "end_offset" : 3,
    "type" : "SYNONYM",
    "position" : 1
  }, {
    "token" : "large",
    "start_offset" : 0,
    "end_offset" : 3,
    "type" : "SYNONYM",
    "position" : 1
  } ]
}
```

On examining the output using the analyze API, we can see that for a particular token that has a synonym, all its synonyms are added to that particular position. This way, we can have a neat, time-efficient implementation of synonyms.

The holy box of search

A holy box of search is a text input box, where you can type all the constraints that you want to search.

For example, if I want to search on a news database for news that has the word "India" in its title, the word "occupation" in its content, is dated between 1990 to 1992, and whose author is Shiv Shankar, I should swiftly be able to search this in the following way:

```
Title:India AND Content:occupation AND
    date:[1900-01-01 TO 1992-01-01] AND author:"Shiv Shankar"
```

For this kind of a search, the query string query is the weapon of our choice.

It gives us a variety of search options, which can be written as plain text. These features are discussed in the next section.

The field search

You can specify a particular field by the `field:value` notation. If you don't specify any field, the search takes place on `_all`, and if you have mentioned the field as the `default_field` option under `query_string_query`, would be taken.

The number/date range search

Using the following notation, you can specify a number range. Some examples are as follows:

- Age above 10: `"age:[10 TO *]`
- Age between 10 and 15: `" age:[10 TO 15]`
- Age excluding 10 and above 10 and below 20: `"age:[10 TO 20]`
- Date between 1990 and 1992: `"date:[1990 TO 1992]`

The phrase search

Phrase search is used in scenarios where you need to check for a match of consecutive words in a field. You can mark a text for phrase search by putting it in double quotes. For example:

```
Content:"occupational hazards"
```

The wildcard search

The wildcard search can also be combined as follows:

```
Content:occup*
```

The regexp search

A Perl-like regex expression is also supported. For example:

```
Content: /indi.*/
```

Boolean operations

Now, let's examine some awesome examples combining all the searches:

```
Query = "india OR asia AND NOT china"
```

As you can see, we utilize Boolean operators such as AND, OR, and NOT and use them to mark Boolean conditions in our query.

As the query string query is very powerful and has a high chance of failure because of the complex formats it supports, it's highly advised that you do not expose this to the end users who are not aware of these operations. The **simple query string** query is a simplified version of the query string query and supports some of its operations.

Words with similar sounds

It would boost user experience if we could map words with similar sounds, such as forgot or forghot. We can use the **phonetic** analyzer for this.

The phonetic analyzer is a community-driven project and is capable of understanding words with similar sounds.

First, we need to install the phonetic analyzer. You can find the code base at

```
https://github.com/elastic/elasticsearch-analysis-phonetic.
```

We can install the plugin using the following command:

```
bin/plugin install elasticsearch/
  elasticsearch-analysis-phonetic/2.4.2
```

Then, we need to create an analyzer out of it:

```
curl -X PUT "http://localhost:9200/my-index" -d '{
  "index": {
    "number_of_shards": 1,
    "number_of_replicas": 1
  },
  "analysis": {
    "filter": {
      "my_metaphone": {
        "type": "phonetic",
        "encoder": "metaphone",
        "replace": false
      }
    },
    "analyzer": {
      "metaphone": {
        "type": "custom",
"tokenizer" : "standard",
        "filter": "my_metaphone"
      }
    }
  }
}'
```

Here, we are creating a filter called my_metaphone and using it to create the
metaphone analyzer. There are many encoders available for phonetic filter,
but here, we have chosen metaphone.

Now, let's see how the metaphone analyzer works. For this, we use the _analyze
API to see the output for various words with the same pronunciation. For the same
purpose, we are choosing the words aamerika, amerika, and America as these three
words have the same pronunciation:

```
curl -XPOST 'localhost:9200/my-index/_analyze?
  analyzer=metaphone&pretty' -d 'aamerika'
{
  "tokens" : [ {
    "token" : "AMRK",
    "start_offset" : 0,
    "end_offset" : 8,
    "type" : "<ALPHANUM>",
    "position" : 1
  }, {
    "token" : "aamerika",
```

```
      "start_offset" : 0,
      "end_offset" : 8,
      "type" : "<ALPHANUM>",
      "position" : 1
    } ]
  }
```

Let's try `amerika`, as shown in the following code:

```
curl -XPOST 'localhost:9200/my-index/_analyze?
  analyzer=metaphone&pretty' -d 'amerika'


{
  "tokens" : [ {
    "token" : "AMRK",
    "start_offset" : 0,
    "end_offset" : 7,
    "type" : "<ALPHANUM>",
    "position" : 1
  }, {
    "token" : "amerika",
    "start_offset" : 0,
    "end_offset" : 7,
    "type" : "<ALPHANUM>",
    "position" : 1
  } ]
}
```

Finally, we try `america` as follows:

```
curl -XPOST 'localhost:9200/my-index/_analyze?
  analyzer=metaphone&pretty' -d 'america'
{
  "tokens" : [ {
    "token" : "AMRK",
    "start_offset" : 0,
    "end_offset" : 7,
    "type" : "<ALPHANUM>",
    "position" : 1
  }, {
    "token" : "america",
    "start_offset" : 0,
    "end_offset" : 7,
    "type" : "<ALPHANUM>",
    "position" : 1
  } ]
}
```

Here, we can see that all the three words were mapped to the same token AMRK on the basis of similar pronunciation.

Substring matching

By now, you would have noticed that only exact word matches are taken as result qualifiers. What if I want an incomplete token or word to be matched?

For example, when I search for titani, it should match against titanium because titani is an incomplete form of titanium.

For this kind of purpose, it would be best to use the **EdgeNGram**-based analyzer.

First let's create the analyzer:

```
curl -X PUT "http://localhost:9200/my-index" -d '{
  "index": {
    "number_of_shards": 1,
    "number_of_replicas": 1
  },
  "analysis": {
    "filter": {
      "ngram": {
        "type": "edgeNgram",
        "min_gram": 1,
"max_gram" : 50
      }
    },
    "analyzer": {
      "NGramAnalyzer": {
        "type": "custom",
        "tokenizer" : "standard",
        "filter": "ngram"
      }
    }
  }
}'
```

Here, we are creating an edge **NGram** filter, which creates substrings of all the tokens from one end of the token with the minimum length of two and the maximum length of 50.

Let's see what its output looks like:

```
curl -XPOST 'localhost:9200/my-index/_analyze?
  analyzer=NGramAnalyzer&pretty' -d 'aamerika'
{
  "tokens" : [ {
    "token" : "a",
    "start_offset" : 0,
    "end_offset" : 8,
    "type" : "word",
    "position" : 1
  }, {
    "token" : "aa",
    "start_offset" : 0,
    "end_offset" : 8,
    "type" : "word",
    "position" : 1
  }, {
    "token" : "aam",
    "start_offset" : 0,
    "end_offset" : 8,
    "type" : "word",
    "position" : 1
  }, {
    "token" : "aame",
    "start_offset" : 0,
    "end_offset" : 8,
    "type" : "word",
    "position" : 1
  }, {
    "token" : "aamer",
    "start_offset" : 0,
    "end_offset" : 8,
    "type" : "word",
    "position" : 1
  }, {
    "token" : "aameri",
    "start_offset" : 0,
    "end_offset" : 8,
    "type" : "word",
    "position" : 1
  }, {
    "token" : "aamerik",
    "start_offset" : 0,
```

```
        "end_offset" : 8,
        "type" : "word",
        "position" : 1
    }, {
        "token" : "aamerika",
        "start_offset" : 0,
        "end_offset" : 8,
        "type" : "word",
        "position" : 1
    } ]
}
```

Summary

We explored various means to improve the user search experience. In all these approaches, we were trying to map the variance of different search patterns into the one the user actually required. We used lowercase, stemming, and synonyms to achieve the same. We went further into the subject and explored the phonetic and **edgeNGram** analyzers, which provided similar functionalities.

In the next chapter, we will see how to use geo information to get better searches and scoring.

7
Spicing Up a Search Using Geo

A geo point refers to the latitude and longitude of a point on Earth. Each location on it has its own unique latitude and longitude. Elasticsearch is aware of geo-based points and allows you to perform various operations on top of it. In many contexts, it's also required to consider a geo location component to obtain various functionalities. For example, say you need to search for all the nearby restaurants that serve Chinese food or I need to find the nearest cab that is free. In some other situation, I need to find to which state a particular geo point location belongs to understand where I am currently standing.

This chapter is modeled such that all the examples mentioned are related to real-life scenarios, of restaurant searching, for better understanding. Here, we take the example of sorting restaurants based on geographical preferences. A number of cases ranging from the simple, such as finding the nearest restaurant, to the more complex case, such as categorization of restaurants based on distance are covered in this chapter.

> What makes Elasticsearch unique and powerful is the fact that you can combine geo operation with any other normal search query to yield results clubbed with both the location data and the query data.

Restaurant search

Let's consider creating a search portal for restaurants. The following are its requirements:

- To find the nearest restaurant with Chinese cuisine, which has the word `ChingYang` in its name.

- To decrease the importance of all restaurants outside city limits.

- To find the distance between the restaurant and current point for each of the preceding restaurant matches.

- To find whether the person is in a particular city's limit or not.

- To aggregate all restaurants within a distance of 10 km. That is, for a radius of the first 10 km, we have to compute the number of restaurants. For the next 10 km, we need to compute the number of restaurants and so on.

Data modeling for restaurants

Firstly, we need to see the aspects of data and model it around a JSON document for Elasticsearch to make sense of the data. A restaurant has a name, its location information, and rating. To store the location information, Elasticsearch has a provision to understand the latitude and longitude information and has features to conduct searches based on it. Hence, it would be best to use this feature.

Let's see how we can do this.

First, let's see what our document should look like:

```
{
    "name" : "Tamarind restaurant",
    "location" : {
        "lat" : 1.10,
        "lon" : 1.54
    }
}
```

Now, let's define the schema for the same:

```
curl -X PUT "http://$hostname:9200/restaurants" -d '{
    "index": {
        "number_of_shards": 1,
        "number_of_replicas": 1
    },
    "analysis":{
```

```
            "analyzer":{
                "flat" : {
                    "type" : "custom",
                    "tokenizer" : "keyword",
                    "filter" : "lowercase"
                }
            }
        }
    }' 


echo
curl -X PUT "http://$hostname:9200/restaurants
  /restaurant/_mapping" -d '{
    "restaurant" : {
    "properties" : {
        "name" : { "type" : "string"  },
        "location" : { "type" : "geo_point", "accuracy" : "1km" }
    }}


}'
```

Let's now index some documents in the index. An example of this would be the `Tamarind restaurant` data shown in the previous section. We can index the data as follows:

```
curl -XPOST 'http://localhost:9200/restaurants/restaurant' -d '{
    "name": "Tamarind restaurant",
    "location": {
        "lat": 1.1,
        "lon": 1.54
    }
}'
```

Likewise, we can index any number of documents. For the sake of convenience, we have indexed only a total of five restaurants for this chapter.

The latitude and longitude should be of this format. Elasticsearch also accepts two other formats (`geohash` and `lat_lon`), but let's stick to this one. As we have mapped the field location to the type `geo_point`, Elasticsearch is aware of what this information means and how to act upon it.

The nearest hotel problem

Let's assume that we are at a particular point where the latitude is 1.234 and the longitude is 2.132. We need to find the nearest restaurants to this location.

For this purpose, the `function_score` query is the best option. We can use the **decay (Gauss)** functionality of the function score query to achieve this:

```
curl -XPOST 'http://localhost:9200/restaurants/_search' -d '{
  "query": {
    "function_score": {
      "functions": [
        {
          "gauss": {
            "location": {
              "scale": "1km",
              "origin": [
                1.231,
                1.012
              ]
            }
          }
        }
      ]
    }
  }
}'
```

Here, we tell Elasticsearch to give a higher score to the restaurants that are nearby the referral point we gave it. The closer it is, the higher is the importance.

The maximum distance covered

Now, let's move on to another example of finding restaurants that are within 10 kms from my current position. Those that are beyond 10 kms are of no interest to me. So, it almost makes up to a circle with a radius of 10 km from my current position, as shown in the following map:

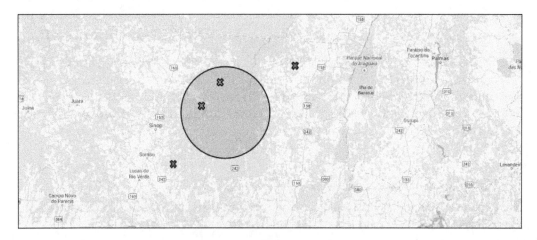

Our best bet here is using a geo distance filter. It can be used as follows:

```
curl -XPOST 'http://localhost:9200/restaurants/_search' -d '{
  "query": {
    "filtered": {
      "filter": {
        "geo_distance": {
          "distance": "100km",
          "location": {
            "lat": 1.232,
            "lon": 1.112
          }
        }
      }
    }
  }
}'
```

Inside the city limits

Next, I need to consider only those restaurants that are inside a particular city limit; the rest are of no interest to me. As the city shown in the following map is rectangle in nature, this makes my job easier:

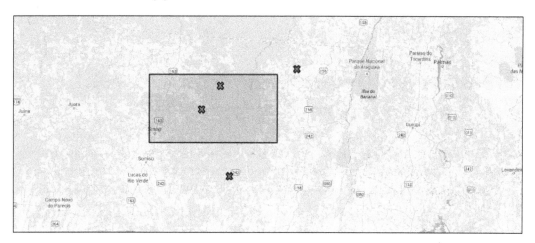

Now, to see whether a geo point is inside a rectangle, we can use the bounding box filter. A rectangle is marked when you feed the top-left point and bottom-right point.

Let's assume that the city is within the following rectangle with the top-left point as *X* and *Y* and the bottom-right point as *A* and *B*:

```
curl -XPOST 'http://localhost:9200/restaurants/_search' -d '{
  "query": {
    "filtered": {
      "query": {
        "match_all": {}
      },
      "filter": {
        "geo_bounding_box": {
          "location": {
            "top_left": {
              "lat": 2,
              "lon": 0
            },
            "bottom_right": {
              "lat": 0,
              "lon": 2
            }
          }
        }
      }
    }
  }
}'
```

Distance values between the current point and each restaurant

Now, consider the scenario where you need to find the distance between the user location and each restaurant. How can we achieve this requirement? We can use scripts; the current geo coordinates are passed to the script and then the query to find the distance between each restaurant is run, as in the following code. Here, the current location is given as (1, 2):

```
curl -XPOST 'http://localhost:9200/restaurants/_search?pretty' -d '{
  "script_fields": {
    "distance": {
      "script": "doc['"'"'location'"'"'].arcDistanceInKm(1, 2)"
    }
  },
  "fields": [
```

```
      "name"
    ],
    "query": {
      "match": {
        "name": "chinese"
      }
    }
  }'
```

We have used the function called `arcDistanceInKm` in the preceding query, which accepts the geo coordinates and then returns the distance between that point and the locations satisfied by the query. Note that the unit of distance calculated is in **kilometers (km)**. You might have noticed a long list of quotes and double quotes before and after `location` in the script mentioned previously. This is the standard format and if we don't use this, it would result in returning the format error while processing.

The distances are calculated from the current point to the filtered hotels and are returned in the `distance` field of response, as shown in the following code:

```
{
  "took" : 3,
  "timed_out" : false,
  "_shards" : {
    "total" : 1,
    "successful" : 1,
    "failed" : 0
  },
  "hits" : {
    "total" : 2,
    "max_score" : 0.7554128,
    "hits" : [ {
      "_index" : "restaurants",
      "_type" : "restaurant",
      "_id" : "AU08uZX6QQuJvMORdWRK",
      "_score" : 0.7554128,
      "fields" : {
        "distance" : [ 112.92927483176413 ],
        "name" : [ "Great chinese restaurant" ]
      }
    }, {
      "_index" : "restaurants",
      "_type" : "restaurant",
      "_id" : "AU08uZaZQQuJvMORdWRM",
      "_score" : 0.7554128,
```

```
            "fields" : {
              "distance" : [ 137.61635969665923 ],
              "name" : [ "Great chinese restaurant" ]
            }
        } ]
     }
  }
```

Note that the distances measured from the current point to the hotels are direct distances and not road distances.

Restaurants out of city limits

One of my friends called me and asked me to join him on his journey to the next city. As we were leaving the city, he was particular that he wants to eat at some restaurant off the city limits, but outside the next city. For this, the requirement was translated to any restaurant that is minimum 15 kms and a maximum of 100 kms from the center of the city. Hence, we have something like a donut in which we have to conduct our search, as show in the following map:

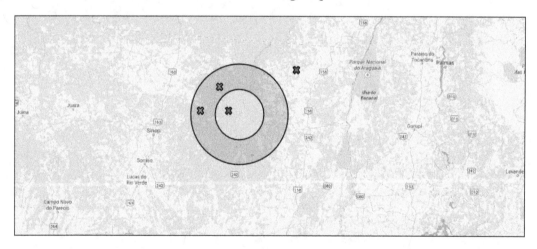

The area inside the donut is a match, but the area outside is not. For this donut area calculation, we have the `geo_distance_range` filter to our rescue. Here, we can apply the minimum distance and maximum distance in the fields `from` and `to` to populate the results, as shown in the following code:

```
curl -XPOST 'http://localhost:9200/restaurants/_search' -d '{
    "query": {
        "filtered": {
            "query": {
                "match_all": {}
```

```
    },
    "filter": {
      "geo_distance_range": {
        "from": "15km",
        "to": "100km",
        "location": {
          "lat": 1.232,
          "lon": 1.112
        }
      }
    }
  }
}'
```

Restaurant categorization based on distance

In an e-commerce solution, to search restaurants, it's required that you increase the searchable characteristics of the application. This means that if we are able to give a snapshot of results other than the top-10 results, it would add to the searchable characteristics of the search. For example, if we are able to show how many restaurants serve Indian, Thai, or other cuisines, it would actually help the user to get a better idea of the result set.

In a similar manner, if we can tell them if the restaurant is near, at a medium distance, or far away, we can really pull a chord in the restaurant search user experience, as shown in the following map:

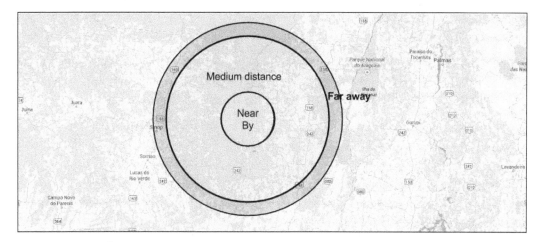

Implementing this is not hard, as we have something called the **distance range aggregation**. In this aggregation type, we can handcraft the range of distance we are interested in and create a bucket for each of them. We can also define the key name we need, as shown in the following code:

```
curl -XPOST 'http://localhost:9200/restaurants/_search' -d '{
  "aggs": {
    "distanceRanges": {
      "geo_distance": {
        "field": "location",
        "origin": "1.231, 1.012",
        "unit": "meters",
        "ranges": [
          {
            "key": "Near by Locations",
            "to": 200
          },
          {
            "key": "Medium distance Locations",
            "from": 200,
            "to": 2000
          },
          {
            "key": "Far Away Locations",
            "from": 2000
          }
        ]
      }
    }
  }
}'
```

In the preceding code, we categorized the restaurants under three distance ranges, which are the nearby hotels (less than 200 meters), medium distant hotels (within 200 meters to 2,000 meters), and the far away ones (greater than 2,000 meters). This logic was translated to the Elasticsearch query using which, we received the results as follows:

```
{
  "took": 44,
  "timed_out": false,
  "_shards": {
    "total": 1,
    "successful": 1,
    "failed": 0
```

```
    },
    "hits": {
      "total": 5,
      "max_score": 0,
      "hits": [

      ]
    },
    "aggregations": {
      "distanceRanges": {
        "buckets": [
          {
            "key": "Near by Locations",
            "from": 0,
            "to": 200,
            "doc_count": 1
          },
          {
            "key": "Medium distance Locations",
            "from": 200,
            "to": 2000,
            "doc_count": 0
          },
          {
            "key": "Far Away Locations",
            "from": 2000,
            "doc_count": 4
          }
        ]
      }
    }
}
```

In the results, we received how many restaurants are there in each distance range indicated by the doc_count field.

Aggregating restaurants based on their nearness

In the previous example, we saw the aggregation of restaurants based on their distance from the current point to three different categories. Now, we can consider another scenario in which we classify the restaurants on the basis of the geohash grids that they belong to. This kind of classification can be advantageous if the user would like to get a geographical picture of how the restaurants are distributed.

Here is the code for a geohash-based aggregation of restaurants:

```
curl -XPOST 'http://localhost:9200/restaurants/_search?pretty' -d '{
  "size": 0,
  "aggs": {
    "DifferentGrids": {
      "geohash_grid": {
        "field": "location",
        "precision": 6
      },
      "aggs": {
        "restaurants": {
          "top_hits": {}
        }
      }
    }
  }
}'
```

You can see from the preceding code that we used the geohash aggregation, which is named as `DifferentGrids` and the precision here, is to be set as 6. The `precision` field value can be varied within the range of 1 to 12, with 1 being the lowest and 12 being the highest reference of precision.

Also, we used another aggregation named `restaurants` inside the `DifferentGrids` aggregation. The `restaurant` aggregation uses the `top_hits` query to fetch the aggregated details from the `DifferentGrids` aggregation, which otherwise, would return only the `key` and `doc_count` values.

So, running the preceding code gives us the following result:

```
{
  "took":5,
  "timed_out":false,
  "_shards":{
    "total":1,
    "successful":1,
    "failed":0
  },
  "hits":{
    "total":5,
    "max_score":0,
    "hits":[

    ]
  },
```

```
"aggregations":{
   "DifferentGrids":{
      "buckets":[
         {
            "key":"s009",
            "doc_count":2,
            "restaurants":{... }
         },
         {
            "key":"s01n",
            "doc_count":1,
            "restaurants":{... }
         },
         {
            "key":"s00x",
            "doc_count":1,
            "restaurants":{... }
         },
         {
            "key":"s00p",
            "doc_count":1,
            "restaurants":{... }
         }
      ]
   }
}
}
```

As we can see from the response, there are four buckets with the key values, which are s009, s01n, s00x, and s00p. These key values represent the different geohash grids that the restaurants belong to. From the preceding result, we can evidently say that the s009 grid contains two restaurants inside it and all the other grids contain one each.

A pictorial representation of the previous aggregation would be like the one shown on the following map:

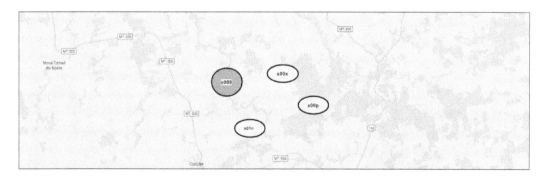

Summary

We found that Elasticsearch can handle geo point and various geo-specific operations. A few geospecific and geopoint operations that we covered in this chapter were searching for nearby restaurants (restaurants inside a circle), searching for restaurants within a range (restaurants inside a concentric circle), searching for restaurants inside a city (restaurants inside a rectangle), searching for restaurants inside a polygon, and categorization of restaurants by the proximity. Apart from these, we can use Kibana, a flexible and powerful visualization tool provided by Elasticsearch for geo-based operations.

Handling Time-based Data

8

In this chapter, we will explore the solutions to the difficulties that we face when we use conventional indexing in Elasticsearch. You would be introduced to the following topics in this chapter:

- Problems encountered using conventionally unplanned indexing data that is time-based
- Indexing time-based data in Elasticsearch
- Overriding defaults for future indices
- Overriding index-level, type-level, and field-level settings
- Conducting high-performance search in time-based data
- Tuning performance of recent data

In the previous chapters, we saw how to index data in Elasticsearch. Now that we have done a pretty basic form of indexing, let's examine the pros of cons of the normal approach. In the indexing approach so far, we saw that when we create an index, we also define the number of shards associated with it. Once we create an index, we can't increase or decrease its number of shards.

Shards, as you may recall, are where our data is contained. However, once we specify the number of shards while index creation, it is not possible to increase or decrease the number at a later point in time. So, this approach is basically fine only if we have a prior idea of how much data is going to be contained in the index we created. Be that as it may, this is not necessarily the case many times. The main issue with this type of indexing comes when the data being indexed is time-based.

Let's explore the problem in detail, that is, when the time-based data comes into picture. Time-based data is where we keep on adding documents with time. Initially, there might not be significant amount of data, but as time progresses, there might be huge volumes of data.

A Twitter-listening tool can make a perfect example of how to demonstrate the issues caused by the normal way of indexing. Suppose we plan to index all the tweets from a geographical location, say US. If we use a single index to store all these tweets, at some point of time, the system will break, as we can't scale beyond the number of shards that the index has defined.

So, we have to find a way to address the previous issues in index creation. The best way to store data would be to create one index per time frame for time data. Here, depending on the volume of data, we can have one index per hour, per day, a week, or even for a month. This facilitates easy data management and also addresses the issues that can be caused due to single indexing in Elasticsearch.

The following figure shows an index creation methodology, where the indices are created and named on a per day basis. Here, in the following example, the naming is done as YYYY-MM-DD, that is, the year-month-day format, with a prefix logstash:

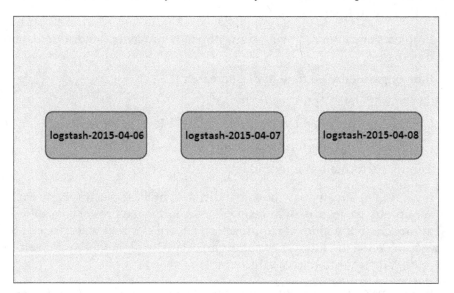

Overriding default mapping and settings in Elasticsearch

In time-based data, we noticed that we create a new index per time frame. Assuming that the index per time frame needs custom settings other than the default ones, it's not possible to create all future indices manually. As Elasticsearch automatically creates missing indices while indexing, with default settings and mappings, we need some mechanism to override the defaults.

Elasticsearch allows us to override index settings, type settings, and even field-level settings based on patterns.

Index template creation

Template creation is one of the most important features in Elasticsearch. It is used extensively with time-based data indexing. The main reason why we employ template creation for indexing is that most of the time, we would use our custom settings and mappings for different sets of data. Index templating allows us define default settings for indices by providing an index name pattern. So, let's assume that we have an index per day and the format is `logstash-YYYY-MM-DD`. Let's say, we want an index with only 2 shards and not 5 shards, which is the default. We can assign a template to the `logstash-*` pattern. Every time a document is inserted and when the index for the document is missing, the pattern will take the default value from the template. Let's see how a template is created:

```
curl -XPUT localhost:9200/_template/logstash -d '{
  "template": "logstash-*",
  "order": 0,
  "settings": {
    "number_of_shards": 2
  },
  "mappings": {
    "logs": {
      "_source": {
        "enabled": false
      }
    }
  }
}'
```

Here, a template named `logstash` is created, where we defined our custom settings and mappings. We defined a `template` field, which defines all index name patterns that it would match against and apply the template settings to. In this example, the settings and mappings will be applied to any index name that matches the `logstash-*` template. That is, if there are indices of the name, `logstash-23-06-2015`, `logstash-master`, and `logstash:server`, the template settings and mapping would be applied to the first-two indices as it matches the pattern defined in our template.

We have an `order` field in the preceding template definition code, which is given the value `0`. The order value sets the priority in which the created template would be preferred by Elasticsearch.

Deleting a template

Templates are identified by their names in Elasticsearch. So, if we want to delete the template named `logstash`, the following code would do:

```
curl -XDELETE localhost:9200/_template/logstash
```

The GET template

Here also, the identification is by name and we can retrieve a template by its name. In our case, it would be:

```
curl -XGET localhost:9200/_template/logstash
```

Multiple matching of templates

It is a very common practice to use multiple templates for the creation of indices in Elasticsearch. You may often ask the question that what happens if there are conflicting settings/mapping in such templates? Let's have a look at such a scenario. Suppose that we have two templates defined as follows:

- template 1:

```
curl -XPUT localhost:9200/_template/logstash1 -d '{
  "template": "logstash-*",
  "order": 0,
  "settings": {
    "number_of_shards": 2
  },
  "mappings": {
    "logs": {
      "_source": {
        "enabled": false
      }
    }
  }
}'
```

- template 2:

```
curl -XPUT localhost:9200/_template/logstash2 -d ' {
  "template": "logs*",
  "order": 1,
  "settings": {
    "number_of_shards": 3
  },
```

```
    "mappings": {
      "logs": {
        "_source": {
          "enabled": false
        }
      }
    }
  }'
```

In this case, the indices' named `logstash-21-04-2015` and `logstash-server` fall under both the templates. However, the settings of the templates `logstash1` and `logstash2` have a conflict in the `number_of_shards` field. So, it would be interesting to figure out which template would Elasticsearch apply to the indices.

In case of multiple templates matching an index name, all the matching template settings would be merged to get the settings for the index that is to be created. In case of collision, the order number would be used to resolve the collision.

As you can see, the `logstash1` template has been defined by an order of 0, while the `logstash2` template has been defined by an order of 1. The lesser the value of the `order` field, the greater the priority. This means that in case of a conflict, the `logstash1` template has a higher priority than `logstash2`, which means that the conflicted field values would be taken from the index with the higher priority and the rest of the fields would be merged.

Overriding default settings for all indices

Now, sometimes, it would be required that all the indices created should have a particular set of mappings/settings.

This can be made easy by creating an index template, which applies for all the indices. For that, we can define the `template` field as *, which would enable the template to apply all its settings/mappings to indices with any name.

An example for such an index template is given as follows:

```
curl -XPUT localhost:9200/_template/forall -d '{
  "template": "*",
  "order": 2,
  "settings": {
    "number_of_shards": 3
  },
  "mappings": {
    "logs": {
      "_all": {
```

```
            "enabled": false
          }
        }
      }
    }'
```

Overriding mapping of all types under an index

Using index templates, we can also override the defaults for types under an index. By default, for all index types, _all would be enabled. This might be a waste of resources in many scenarios. In a template, we can define the mapping for the types whose name is known and the defaults for any index type that will be autocreated in future.

An example for this would be:

```
curl -XPUT 'localhost:9200/data-index' -d '{
  "settings": {
    "number_of_shards": 3,
    "number_of_replicas": 0
  },
  "mappings": {
    "_default_": {
      "_all": {
        "enabled": false
      }
    },
    "type1": {
      "_all": {
        "enabled": true
      }
    }
  }
}'
```

Here, we have an index named data-index. Let's say there are three types under the index data-index, named type1, type2, and type3 and for type1, we need to enable the _all field. In the previous case, we by default, disabled the _all field. In order to enable the _all field in type1, we mention it separately and specify enabled as true.

Now with this setting, other than type1, _all would be disabled for all other types.

Overriding default field settings

On a document indexing, if a field is not defined in the mapping, the type of the field is "guessed" based on the data. This works fine, but in many scenarios, we might need to override this behavior. The best example of this would be the time field with custom format.

Dynamic templates are used for dynamic mapping when we need to add new variables on the fly. The dynamic template allows us to define the mappings of the newly generated fields. The mappings can be applied to the newly generated fields on the basis of datatype or field name.

A sample code for such a dynamic template is given as follows:

```
curl -XPUT 'localhost:9200/data-index' -d ' {
  "mappings": {
    "my_type": {
      "dynamic_templates": [
        {
          "customdate": {
            "match": "date_*",
            "match_mapping_type": "string",
            "mapping": {
              "type": "date",
              "format": "yyyy-MM-dd HH:mm:ss||yyyy-MM-dd"
            }
          }
        },
        {
          "customstring": {
            "match": "*",
            "match_mapping_type": "string",
            "mapping": {
              "type": "string",
              "analyzer": "my-analyzer"
            }
          }
        }
      ]
    }
  }
}'
```

In the preceding sample code, we defined two templates named `customdate` and `customstring` for string fields.

What `customdate` does is that it checks all the fields starting with `date_*`. The matching fields are then given the mapping type `date`, which has a specific format defined to it. This in effect is filtering out the `date_*` field to the date format.

Likewise, in the `customstring` template, `match` is defined for `*`, that is, all the fields, and it would apply the mappings to all the fields. The mapping can use any analyzer for this purpose, even the custom ones we created.

The templates are checked in order of their occurrence. Since `customdate` is put first, the fields with `date_*` are mapped first and only then, the `customstring` template is checked.

Searching for time-based data

The peculiar nature of querying time-based data is that, it's mostly time oriented. In most of the queries, there would be a definite time range mostly pointing to the recent data. Let's see how we can take advantage of this in searching.

In the previous section, we saw how to make custom indices for time-based data using templates and how to override the settings and mappings. The most important application, as we saw in the preceding section, is the modeling of indices of our interests for querying. This means that, we can select specific indices from our entire pool of time-based indices and do operations on a selected few.

Suppose that we have a number of `logstash` indices named after the week that they were created in. So, in effect for a year, say 2014, there would be a total of 52 indices. Assume that we also created the indices' name in the format `logstash-YYYY-WW`, that is, the year-week number format. So, a sample index would have the name `logstash-2014-21`, which means that the index was created for the data of the 21st week of 2014.

Let's see a real-time scenario and understand how this work. Let's assume that there is one index per day in which the index names are of the pattern `logstash-YYYY-MM-DD`. Now, let's see how we can run a query that wants all the documents that have the company field as `cisco` for the last 3 days:

```
POST /logstash-*/_search
{
  "query": {
    "bool": {
      "must": [
        {
          "range": {
            "created_at": {
              "gt": "now-3d",
```

```
          "lt": "now"
        }
      }
    },
    {
      "term": {
        "company": "cisco"
      }
    }
  ]
      }
    }
  }
```

As you would have noticed, we are running the query on the entire set of indices and not just on the one that we need. Hence, we are unnecessarily wasting bandwidth on a search. A good workaround would be to select only the indices where we want to search.

Hence, the preceding query can be remodeled in a more efficient way, as follows (assuming that today's date is 2015-03-05):

```
POST /logstash-2015-03-05,logstash-2015-03-04,
    logstash-2015-03-03/_search
{
  "query": {
    "bool": {
      "must": [
        {
          "range": {
            "created_at": {
              "gt": "now-3d",
              "lt": "now"
            }
          }
        },
        {
          "term": {
            "company": "cisco"
          }
        }
      ]
    }
  }
}
```

Here, by making sure that we only search for the required indices, we have achieved a greater performance.

Archiving time-based data

While dealing with time-based data, it is often noticed that the most useful data is that of the present. This makes the old data less relevant for our purposes. So as time progresses, the relevancy of past data falls very rapidly and the data we indexed exists without being used in the clusters. This situation is not very resource friendly, as there would be much unused data stored for no or less purpose.

We can visualize different levels of archiving, as follows:

1. Keep the hottest index in the machines that have good hardware (shard filtering).
2. Run the optimized API on indices where writing is done.
3. Close indices that are not required for instant search.
4. Take a snapshot and archive older indices.
5. Finally, remove indices that are no longer required.

Shard filtering

With time-based data, recent indices are more frequently used or are more relevant. In other words, at a given time, the data flowing would use some specific index based on the day, week, or month. This index would be the target for all the new documents and most of the queries would also hit the same index. So, it is a good idea to allocate the best resource for the node that contains our heavily used index.

The problem in this approach is that it would be difficult for Elasticsearch to recognize which node we allocated for the heavily used index. In order to make Elasticsearch understand which node, we can specify tags to the node as it is initiated or started. This can be defined in the configuration file of Elasticsearch as shown:

```
./bin/elasticsearch -node.memory 16G
```

Here, `memory` is an arbitrary key; we can give it any name we want. These key-value pairs act as identifiers for a set of nodes. Hence, we can group different nodes under various values of the key `best_node`. All nodes having the same memory value come under one group. Using this approach, we can manually group machines based on their hardware.

Suppose that we have indexes named `logstash-02-07-2015` and `logstash-02-06-2015`. Let's say, the first index is our current index and we need to allocate the node having the index with the best resource. Here, the second index `logstash-02-06-2015` is an old one and we are not heavily using it for time being.

Here is how we make Elasticsearch understand the same:

```
PUT / logstash-02-07-2015
{
  "settings": {
    "index.routing.allocation.include.memory ": "16G"
  }
}
```

In the preceding code, for the creation of the index, we specified that the data flow should be to the node that has the `best_node" : 16G"` tag, which is our best resource.

We saw how to move the data to the best node; now, as we mentioned earlier, older data can be less useful and we can see how the old indices can be moved to lesser- or medium-resource nodes.

First, define the tags for the nodes (here, with lesser resources):

```
./bin/elasticsearch –node.memory 8G
```

Then, in our example, the old index is `logstash-02-06-2015`. Now update the settings for that index as shown:

```
POST / logstash-02-06-2015/_settings
{
    "index.routing.allocation.include.memory" : "8G"
}
```

Now, the index `logstash-02-06-2015` is moved to the nodes that match the `memory" : "8G"` tags. This way, the current index, which is write heavy and read heavy are allocated to machines that have.

A graphical representation of what happens in the shard allocation is shown in the following figure:

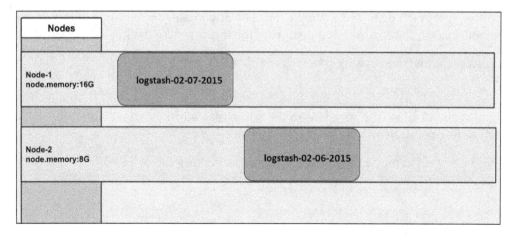

Running the optimized API on indices where writing is done

In time data indexing, the writing for the previous indices would be done and it would mostly be read only. So, it makes sense to convert multiple segments of those indices to a single segment. A single segment has advantage of resource utilization and performance. It's a good idea to optimize indices on a single segment, but then, if it's a index where documents are still flowing, it's a bad idea.

Now, we can run a forced merge operation using the following HTTP request:

```
POST / logstash-02-06-2015/_optimize?max_num_segments=1
```

As you can see, we used the optimize API (_optimize) in the preceding code. The optimize API would force a shard to merge its segments with the number we assign to max_num_segments.

In this case, we defined the maximum number of segments to be used as 1. The general practice is to set the maximum number of segments as 1 because it will use fewer resources and the search operations would also be a lot faster.

Closing older indices

As the time progresses, the documents residing in the older indices will be even less utilized to the level that they might not even be accessed. These indices would use our CPU, main memory, and other resources as they reside in the disk in their nodes. This situation is not a healthy one, as we are simply giving away our resources for the unused or unaccessed data. Elasticsearch provides us a provision to manage this situation by letting us "close" old indices.

Closing an index means that the index would still remain in the cluster with no resource except the disk space being used. The advantage of closing an index is that it is much easier to reopen it than restoring the index from a backup.

We can close that index using the close API:

```
POST / logstash-02-06-2015/_close
```

As mentioned earlier, the specified index will be stored in the disk, but all the read/write operations would be blocked for it.

In case we want to reopen the index, we can do so using the open API:

```
POST / logstash-02-06-2015/_open
```

Snapshot creation and restoration of indices

There would be very old indices that store time-based data and it will be better if they are removed from our ecosystem, so that we can utilize the disk space that they were occupying. Such indices can be kept separately in a shared disk or some other third-party long term storage services in case we want to access them in future. The advantage of having such backups is that the data is never truly lost, as we can recover those indices from the backups we have.

Elasticsearch provides the snapshot-restore API for the previously mentioned purposes. Let's see how to create a snapshot.

Repository creation

Prior to creating a snapshot, it is necessary for us to register a repository in Elasticsearch. This can be done as follows:

```
PUT/_snapshot/index_backup
{
  "type": "fs",
  "settings": {
    "compress": "true",
    "location": "/mount/backups"
  }
}
```

Here we can see the `type` field defined with the value `fs`. This means that we are creating the repository in the filesystem. If we use an external storage plugin, such as AWS, the type value should be fed as `s3` and the settings would also change accordingly. An example for an AWS snapshot repository would be:

```
PUT /_snapshot/backup_s3
{
  "type": "s3",
  "settings": {
    "bucket": "s3_backup",
    "region": "eu-west-1"
  }
}
```

Snapshot creation

We saw the creation and registration of a repository in the previous section; now, we can move forward to the creation of snapshots.

Creating a snapshot named `snap01` in the `index_backup` repository can be done by the following command:

```
PUT /_snapshot/index_backup/snap01
```

We can also use the `wait_for_completion` parameter along with the preceding command as follows:

```
PUT /_snapshot/index_backup/snap01?wait_for_completion=true
```

The `wait_for_completion` parameter if set to `true`, will wait till the snapshot is created and then only the request would return. Whereas, the `false` value would return the request immediately while allowing the snapshot creation to be done in the background. The default value for `wait_for_completion` is taken as `false`, even if the parameter is not mentioned during snapshot creation.

Snapshot creation on specific indices

When we create a snapshot, by default, it would take backups of all the up and running indices in the cluster. This behavior may be not fine in some cases, as we would need backups of specific indices. This can be done by the following command:

```
PUT /_snapshot/index_backup/snap01
{
    "indices": "logstash-20-06-2015,logstash-20-05-2015",
    "ignore_unavailable": "true"
}
```

Here, the snapshot `snap01` would contain the backups of the data in the indices `logstash-20-06-2015` and `logstash-20-05-2015`.

The `ignore_unavailable` parameter when set to `true`, would ignore unavailability of the index/indices while snapshots are created.

Restoring a snapshot

The snapshot we created named `snap01` can be restored by the following command:

```
POST /_snapshot/index_backup/snap01/_restore
```

By default, all the indices in the snapshot are restored through this method.

Restoring multiple indices

The replacement of selective indices is also supported as follows:

```
POST /_snapshot/index_backup/snap01/_restore
{
  "indices": " logstash-20-06-2015,logstash-20-05-2015",
  "ignore_unavailable": "true"
}
```

An existing index can only be restored if it is closed and has the same number of shards as the index in the snapshot.

The curator

Curator is tool developed in Python by the Elasticsearch community to curate or manage the time-based indices in Elasticsearch. The main aim of curator is to run operations on time-based modeled indices. Say, we want to optimize all indices older than today. We will need to query and understand which all indices come under this condition and then, we need to run the command for each of the index. This might be a time-consuming process. For this, we can use curator and ask it to do tasks on time-based indices for us. For instance, we can tell curator to delete/optimize indices older than a day.

Curator understands various time-based index name formats once they are given as command-line arguments. Using the same, you can issue various commands.

By using curator, we can perform the previously mentioned operations on the index, such as:

- Shard allocation
- Opening and closing of indices
- Optimization
- Snapshot creation

Shard allocation using curator

As seen earlier, the task of allocation of good machines to the desired index can be done using the curator tool, shown as follows:

```
curator  --host <IP> allocation --rule memory=16G indices
--timestring '%Y-%M-%D' --prefix "logstash-" --newer-than 2 --time-
unit days
```

Here, we are telling curator to move all the indexes that are newer than the past 2 days to nodes that have memory attribute as the 16G value. With this process, the latest indices would be moved to better hardware, as follows:

```
curator  --host <IP> allocation --rule ram=8G indices    --timestring
'%Y-%M-%D' --prefix "logstash-"  --older-than  2 --time-unit days
```

We also need to run the preceding command to make sure that the rest of indices are moved to normal nodes that have only 8GB main memory.

Opening and closing of indices

The opening or closing of indices can also be done using curator. An example of this would be:

```
curator  --host <IP> close   --timestring '%Y-%M-%D' --prefix
"logstash-"  --older-than  10 --time-unit days
```

Here, we are closing all indices older than 10 days, so that they won't eat up too much of the hardware resource.

Optimization

The optimization or forced merging of all the indices with the prefix logstash- into a single shard can be done using the following command:

```
curator --host 10<IP> optimize --max_num_segments 1 -prefix
"logstash-"  --older-than  1 --time-unit days
```

Here, we setting a number of segments for all indices older than today.

Summary

In this chapter, we saw the problems caused by normal index creation, while indexing time data. You also learned how to overcome these difficulties by creating templates to create indices and overriding the default mappings and settings of indices.

We also saw how to make selective indices to be included for querying, and understood the benefits of such a feature. We also familiarized ourselves with some methods through which the old time data can be handled, as follows:

- Migration of indices
- Shard allocation
- Optimizing indices
- Closing of indices
- Creating snapshots of indices

In this chapter, we saw the curator tool developed for the index management in Elasticsearch, which can be used to do most of the preceding operations.

Index

A

aggregation
  about 28
  terms aggregation 29
algorithmic approach 124
analysis process 22
analyzers
  about 6, 7
  character filters 6
  custom analyzers, creating 9
  readymade analyzers 10-12
  setting 6
  token filters 6
  tokenizers 6
analyzing, of tokens 6
autocomplete
  about 40
  characteristics 42
  finite state automata (FST), using 40, 41
  implementing, in hotel suggester 42-45

B

Boolean operations
  performing 129
boost query
  using 60

C

case-insensitive search
  enabling 116, 117
category filter
  implementing 32

character filters
  about 6-8
  HTML stripper 8
  mapping char filter 8
consistent pagination
  with scroll API 40
content match
  title match, prioritizing 119
curator
  about 163
  for closing indices 164
  for opening indices 164
  for optimizing indices 164
  for shard allocation 164
cURL
  about 2
  data, specifying in command line 3
  data, specifying in file 4
  URL 2
custom analyzers
  creating 9

D

data modeling 20-24
date range filter
  implementing 30
decay (Gauss) functionality 138
dictionary-based approach 124
distance range aggregation 144
doc ID 3
documents
  searching, with match query 26
DSL (domain-specific language) 25

E

Ebola outbreak records, sorting
about 53
by boost match in title field over
description 53-55
by certain symptoms over others 60-63
by healthy people from unhealthy
locations 68, 69
by medical journals for different
interns 63, 64
by medical journals from closest place to
outbreak 65
by most recent Ebola report on healthy
patients 58, 59
by most recent medical journals 57
by order in which symptoms
appeared 69, 70
from unhealthy places near Ebola
outbreak 66, 67
EdgeNGram-based analyzer
using 132
Elasticsearch
about 1, 2
deploying 2
features 3
URL 2
Elasticsearch server
communicating with 3
index-type mapping 5
replicas 4, 5
shards 4, 5
e-mail search
enabling, inside text 117, 118
explain flag 50

F

filter
and query, selecting between 24, 25
category filter, implementing 32
date range filter, implementing 30
implementing, in Elasticsearch 33
prize range filter, implementing 31, 32
usage 25
finite state automata (FST)
about 40
using 40, 41

flight ticket analytics
correlation, checking for passenger's
purpose of visit 111-114
correlation, checking for passenger's
sex 111-114
correlation, checking for passenger's
ticket type 111-114
correlation of departure and arrival of
flights 100-102
correlation of ticket type with time 103, 104
distribution of travel duration 105-107
index creation 95, 96
male and female distribution,
of passengers 97, 99
mapping creation 95, 96
most preferred hour, for booking
tickets 107-109
most preferred weekday, for travel 109-111
requisites 97
scenario 94
ticket booking trends 99
function query
using 57, 65
function score query
using 54, 67, 68

G

geo point 135

H

has_child query/the has_child filter 81
has_parent filter/the has_parent query 81
head UI 16, 17
highlighting
using 14, 15
holy box of search
about 128
field search 128
number/date range search 128
phrase search 128
Regexp search 129
wildcard search 129
horizontal scaling 4
hotel suggester
autocomplete, implementing 42-45

stemmer token filter 9
stop word token filter 8
tokenizers
about 6
lowercase tokenizer 8
shingle tokenizer 8
whitespace tokenizer 8
tokens 5
top_children query 82
Twitter-listening tool 150

U

UAX Email URL tokenizer 118
URL link search
enabling, inside text 117, 118

V

vertical scaling 4

W

whitespace tokenizer 8

Z

Zomato 42

Thank you for buying
Elasticsearch Blueprints

About Packt Publishing

Packt, pronounced 'packed', published its first book, *Mastering phpMyAdmin for Effective MySQL Management*, in April 2004, and subsequently continued to specialize in publishing highly focused books on specific technologies and solutions.

Our books and publications share the experiences of your fellow IT professionals in adapting and customizing today's systems, applications, and frameworks. Our solution-based books give you the knowledge and power to customize the software and technologies you're using to get the job done. Packt books are more specific and less general than the IT books you have seen in the past. Our unique business model allows us to bring you more focused information, giving you more of what you need to know, and less of what you don't.

Packt is a modern yet unique publishing company that focuses on producing quality, cutting-edge books for communities of developers, administrators, and newbies alike. For more information, please visit our website at www.packtpub.com.

About Packt Open Source

In 2010, Packt launched two new brands, Packt Open Source and Packt Enterprise, in order to continue its focus on specialization. This book is part of the Packt Open Source brand, home to books published on software built around open source licenses, and offering information to anybody from advanced developers to budding web designers. The Open Source brand also runs Packt's Open Source Royalty Scheme, by which Packt gives a royalty to each open source project about whose software a book is sold.

Writing for Packt

We welcome all inquiries from people who are interested in authoring. Book proposals should be sent to author@packtpub.com. If your book idea is still at an early stage and you would like to discuss it first before writing a formal book proposal, then please contact us; one of our commissioning editors will get in touch with you.

We're not just looking for published authors; if you have strong technical skills but no writing experience, our experienced editors can help you develop a writing career, or simply get some additional reward for your expertise.

Building a Search Server with Elasticsearch [Video]

ISBN: 978-1-78328-415-3   Duration: 01:53 hrs

Build a fully featured and scalable search UI with Elasticsearch

1. Start building your own search engine with Elasticsearch, from setup to ingestion and querying.

2. Set up an Elasticsearch cluster and a full search interface in AngularJS, all in one comprehensive project.

3. Implement search features such as highlighting, filters, and autocomplete, and build a robust search engine.

Mastering Elasticsearch
Second Edition

ISBN: 978-1-78355-379-2   Paperback: 434 pages

Further your knowledge of the Elasticsearch server by learning more about its internals, querying, and data handling

1. Understand Apache Lucene and Elasticsearch's design and architecture.

2. Design your index, configure it, and distribute it, not only with assumptions, but with the underlying knowledge of how it works.

3. Improve your user search experience with Elasticsearch functionality and learn how to develop your own Elasticsearch plugins.

Please check **www.PacktPub.com** for information on our titles

ElasticSearch Cookbook
Second Edition

ElasticSearch Cookbook
Second Edition

ISBN: 978-1-78355-483-6   Paperback: 472 pages

Over 130 advanced recipes to search, analyze, deploy, manage, and monitor data effectively with ElasticSearch

1. Deploy and manage simple ElasticSearch nodes as well as complex cluster topologies.

2. Write native plugins to extend the functionalities of ElasticSearch to boost your business.

3. Packed with clear, step-by-step recipes to walk you through the capabilities of ElasticSearch.

Elasticsearch Server
Second Edition

Elasticsearch Server
Second Edition

ISBN: 978-1-78398-052-9   Paperback: 428 pages

A practical guide to building fast, scalable, and flexible search solutions with clear and easy-to-understand examples

1. Learn about the fascinating functionality of Elasticsearch such as data indexing, data analysis, and dynamic mapping.

2. Fine-tune Elasticsearch and understand its metrics using its API and available tools, and see how it behaves in complex searches.

3. A hands-on tutorial that walks you through all the features of Elasticsearch in an easy-to-understand way, with examples that will help you become an expert in no time.

Please check **www.PacktPub.com** for information on our titles

www.ingramcontent.com/pod-product-compliance
Lightning Source LLC
LaVergne TN
LVHW081342050326
832903LV00024B/1268